Do it yourself!

Y0-BDG-213

It doesn't necessarily take a highly trained service technician to make most repairs on an appliance. This book shows you just how easy it can be to repair your own washer. Whether you're an avid do-it-yourselfer or just a beginner, the step-by-step photo instructions and detailed explanations will help you perform the majority of washer repairs you're likely to encounter.

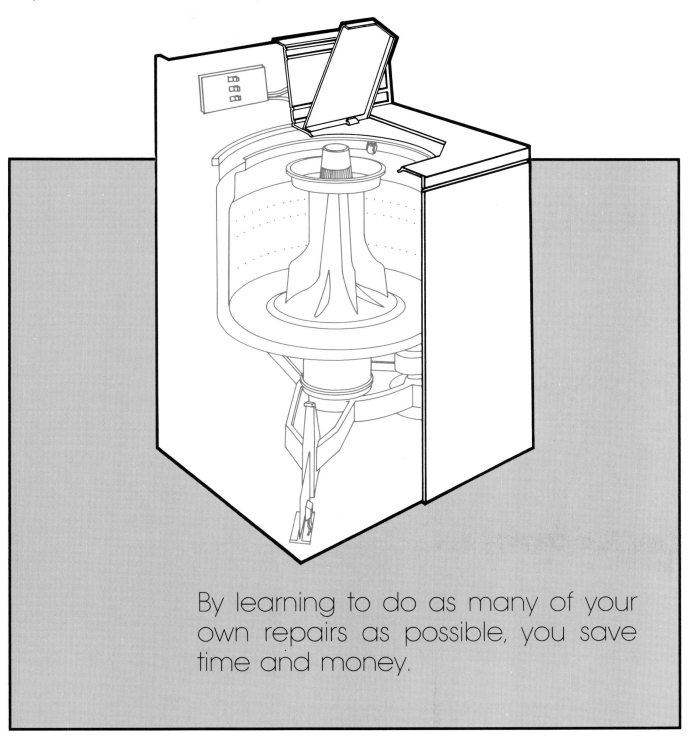

By learning to do as many of your own repairs as possible, you save time and money.

Safety information: Automatic washers are complex electromechanical appliances. Any attempt to repair your washer may, if improperly performed, result in personal injury and property damage. General Electric Company cannot be responsible for the interpretation of this manual, nor can it assume any liability in connection with its use. For more detailed safety information see page 2 of this manual.

If your appliance is still under warranty: Before you attempt any repairs, check to see if your appliance is covered under warranty. If you or any unauthorized service technician tries to repair an appliance under warranty, the warranty may be voided.

Step-By-Step Repair Manual for General Electric and Hotpoint Washers
General Electric Co.

© 1985 by General Electric Co.
Appliance Park
Louisville, KY 40225

All rights reserved. No part of this book may be reproduced in any form or by any means without permission in writing from General Electric Co.

Contents

Note: Pages 1 through 7 contain important information. Be sure to carefully read these pages before you begin any repair procedures.

How to use this manual

General Electric Company has recognized the growing need for the homeowner to perform as many of the service operations as possible around the house. Consequently, we have prepared this manual to provide the typical homeowner with the information necessary to perform the majority of washer repairs. This manual is written in an easy to follow, step-by-step, photo guide format to instruct you how to do your own repairs.

Before you begin your repair

It is important that before you begin any repair or diagnosis on your washer you take the time to read the general information on pages 2 through 7. By acquiring a basic understanding of washer repair and important safety information, you'll be a step ahead on diagnosing and remedying the problem.

Problem Diagnostic Charts

When a problem does occur, refer to the Problem Diagnostic Chart section of the manual (pages 7-15). These charts will help you pinpoint your trouble by listing possible causes from the most likely to the least common cause. The charts will refer you to the repair procedures (pages 16-96) that use photography and illustrations to show you step-by-step how to remedy the problem. Be sure to read the entire repair procedure carefully before attempting any work.

Glossary of Terms

If you find a term you don't understand, you may find it listed in the Glossary of Terms listed at the end of this manual (pages 106-109). Also, don't forget to use the index as a reference when searching for various information.

Read Your *Use and Care Book*

After you have read the introductory sections in this manual, you may want to re-read the *Use and Care Book* that accompanies your washer. The *Use and Care Book* can tell you how to remedy many problems that aren't due to equipment faults, such as overloading and too low water heater temperature. You may just discover that your washer has useful features you've forgotten.

Preventive Maintenance

When you have completed your repair, the Preventive Maintenance section (page 98) can help you obtain the best results from your General Electric or Hotpoint washer. Preventive maintenance is a vital key to long life for your washer. The few minutes you invest in caring for your washer properly can save you a great deal of time and trouble.

What repairs are covered?

Although General Electric Company has introduced hundreds of washer models through the years, similarities in basic components allow this manual to cover most common repairs. Some procedures may not apply to your washer; they may be applicable only for a particular brand (General Electric or Hotpoint), or model type. For instance, your model will have either a single-speed clutch or a two-speed clutch, but it will not have both. The component being repaired may also vary somewhat with different washer models, such as a smaller handwash agitator used on some models. Major differences between models will be noted in the repair procedure.

Safety information

Automatic washers are complex electromechanical appliances. Any attempt to repair your washer may, if improperly performed, result in personal injury and property damage. General Electric Company cannot be responsible for the interpretation of this manual, nor can it assume any liability in connection with its use.

Safety precautions
To minimize the risk of personal injury or property damage it is important that the following safe servicing practices be observed.

---

1. **Be sure you are operating your washer properly. Read carefully the *Use and Care Book* and *User Instruction Sheet* that come with your washer.**

2. **Know the location of your washer's circuit breakers or fuses. Clearly mark all switches and fuses for quick reference. Your washer must be operated on a separate circuit with a 15 or 20 amp time-delay fuse or circuit breaker. No other electrical device should be operated on this circuit when the washer is in use. If you are unfamiliar with circuit breakers and fuses, please refer to Procedure #1: Inspecting Circuit Breakers and Fuses.**

3. **None of the repairs or tests in this manual requires voltage to be applied to the washer for testing. Before servicing your washer, turn all washer controls OFF. Disconnect the power supply at the distribution panel by removing the fuse or switching off the circuit breaker. Unplug the washer before inspecting, testing, or removing any access panel.**

4. **Be careful when handling access panels, washer parts, or any components which may have sharp edges. Avoid placing your hand into any areas of the washer which you cannot first visually inspect for sharp edges.**

5. If replacement wire is required, use only appliance wire having the same temperature and gauge rating as the wire you are replacing.

6. **Never interfere with or bypass the operation of any switch, component or feature of an automatic washer. Safety devices included with your washer, such as the lid switch, inlet air break, shields, and overflow tube, must never be removed or altered.**

7. **Use only replacement parts of the same size and capacity as the original part. If you have any questions, contact your authorized local appliance parts dealer.**

8. **Before reconnecting the power supply, make sure no uninsulated wires or terminals are touching the cabinet. Electrical wiring and grounds must be correctly reconnected and secured away from sharp edges and moving parts. All panels and covers should be reinstalled before the washer is plugged in.**

9. **When replacing any washer component, be sure any green wires are reconnected securely in their original positions to avoid danger of shock or short circuit.**

10. **To prevent burns from hot water or water spills, turn faucets off before removing any hoses. Be careful when removing hoses that any residual hot water in the hose does not leak onto you. Be sure that all hoses are properly connected, are not pinched or stressed, and are clear of all moving washer parts.**

11. **Hydrogen gas can be produced and can build up in a water heater if you have not used hot water for a period of two weeks or more. HYDROGEN GAS CAN BE EXPLOSIVE UNDER THESE CIRCUMSTANCES. To prevent possible damage or injury, run hot water from the kitchen for several minutes before using your washer or any other appliance connected to a hot water system that has not been in use. This will allow any hydrogen to escape. If the gas is present, you may hear a slight hissing or sputtering noise from the faucet as the water begins to flow. Do not smoke or allow any open flame near the faucet at this time.**

12. Carefully read through the entire repair procedure for a specific repair before attempting the job. If you don't fully understand the repair procedure or doubt your ability to complete it, call a qualified service technician.

13. **Throughout this manual additional safety precautions dealing with specific repair procedures will be presented. This information should be read carefully.**

Parts information

Obtaining replacement parts

If you're going to the time and trouble of repairing your appliance, it is important that you get the correct replacement part. First, be sure you have the complete model number for your appliance when ordering replacement parts. Even if you take in the original part, a salesperson may not be able to supply the correct replacement part without your complete model number. Second, to assure proper fit and performance, use Genuine General Electric Renewal Parts.

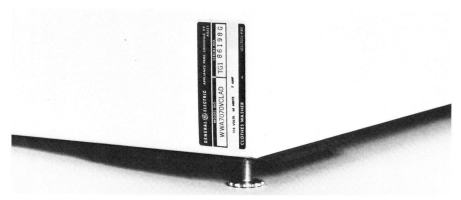

The model specification plate is mounted on the lower left side of the washer cabinet.

Finding your model number

The model and serial numbers of your washer are stamped on a metal model specification plate. On most General Electric and Hotpoint washers, you'll find the model specification plate on the left side of the cabinet.

The complete model number must be used when ordering exact replacement parts. Be sure to copy this number correctly and record it on page 97 of this manual for future reference.

General Electric washer specification plate

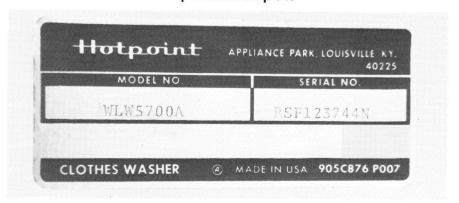

Hotpoint washer specification plate

Genuine GE Renewal Parts

All parts are not created equal when it comes to your General Electric or Hotpoint washer. Some non-General Electric parts may require extra brackets and adaptors to make them fit. Others may not be designed for the exact electrical specifications of your washer and, as a result, may cause substandard performance. With Genuine GE Renewal Parts you are assured a proper fit and performance match for the original part--an assurance that's backed in writing with a one-year limited warranty.

For your convenience in obtaining parts, General Electric has company-owned parts stores and authorized parts dealers throughout the country. To find the outlet nearest you, look in the Yellow Pages under major headings, "Appliances--Household--Major" or "Washers", then subheads, "Service & Repair" or "Supplies & Parts". If you are unable to find where GE parts are sold in your area, call The GE Answer Center® consumer information service toll free 800-626-2000 for assistance.

Some dealers feature the

Genuine General Electric Renewal Parts are backed by a one-year limited warranty to assure you proper fit and performance.

Quick Fix® system of common GE replacement parts and parts kits. Designed specifically for do-it-yourselfers, Quick Fix® parts come in clearly marked packages complete with hardware and step-by-step replacement instructions.

Whether it's the Quick Fix® system or the regular GE line of parts, you should insist on the performance and quality of Genuine General Electric Renewal Parts. After all, if you're investing time and money to care for your appliance, it's better to do it right the first time and not chance problems later from using an unsuitable part.

How your electric washer operates

The purpose of this section is to give you some basic information on how an automatic washer operates, because the more you know about the operation of your washer, the easier it will be to understand the causes and solutions to a problem. For example, in order to wash your clothes, you set the controls to the desired cycle, temperature, and water level. But what causes the machine to time its cycles correctly and fill with the desired amount of water? Knowing basic answers to these questions will make it easier for you to handle repairs. Let's take a closer look at how your washer operates.

Washers may vary in appearance and complexity, but most operate in the same way.

Basically, all washers fill, agitate, spin, fill again, agitate, then spin dry. The most widely used, the top loader, has a large-bladed agitator that oscillates in the middle of the clothes basket, forcing the water and detergent through the fabric.

The operating panel, or console, projects above the washer and houses the timer, water temperature switch, and water level switch. The timer is the heart of the washer and typically has three basic parts: the knob, the

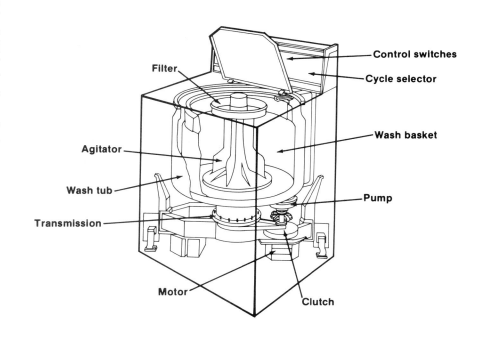

switch section, and the timer motor. Together they control the timing of the various cycles and maintain correct sequence. The timer motor drives a set of cams which turn tiny switches on and off.

All washers have switches that

control such functions as water temperature, water level, and motor speed. Depending on the model, external switches (those manually operated from outside the machine) can be pushbutton, rotary (turning dial), or toggle (like a light switch).

Models covered

Over the years, General Electric and Hotpoint have produced hundreds of various washer models. Repairs on most models are similar, so most problems that may arise with your washer are likely to be covered in this manual.

Exception: This manual does not cover repairs to compact washers (washers less than the normal 27 inch width).

Standard capacity washer

Large capacity washer

Washer features

General Electric and Hotpoint washers are designed to meet various washday needs. They have a wide variety of performance features to provide quality care for all washable fabrics.

Washers can be either standard or large capacity, and may feature an array of cycles, wash speeds, temperature selections, water level settings, and dispenser devices. Some models also offer a concealed Handwash® control system which has a special agitator concealed beneath the regular agitator. This Handwash™ gentle agitator is designed to wash small delicate loads of lightly soiled items.

Washer interiors are constructed with a durable, fired-on porcelain enamel tub that is resistant to stains, scratches, and rust.

Problem diagnostic charts

How to use the problem diagnostic charts

The problem diagnostic charts help you with one of the most difficult tasks in do-it-yourself repairs...locating the possible causes and solutions to your problem. Before using the charts, make note of the problem you are experiencing with your washer. Keen observation can often lead you to the area where the problem lies. Watch for anything that deviates from normal operation. Note everything that is or is not working. Once you have identified a problem, then you can begin to solve it by referring to the Problem Diagnostic Charts.

Each page of the Problem Diagnostic Charts has four columns of information: (1) **Problem**; (2) **Possible Cause**; (3) **Repair Procedure**; and (4) **Skill Level**. The first column, **PROBLEM**, lists examples of problems you may encounter with your washer. In the second column, there is a list of **POSSIBLE CAUSES** that may be the reason for the problem. The possible causes for each problem are listed in the order in which they might be expected to occur, from the most likely to the least likely. A **REPAIR PROCEDURE** for each possible cause is listed in column three. Repair procedure information refers you to a course of action to remedy the possible cause of your washer problem.

The final column, **SKILL LEVEL**, indicates a skill level rating for each repair task. This rating will help you decide which repairs you feel confident of completing.

NOTE: The problems listed below are numbered exactly as they appear in the PROBLEM column of the Problem Diagnostic Charts.

Washer problems

1. Washer will not operate
2. Washer will not fill
3. Washer will not stop filling
4. Washer leaking water on floor
5. Washer will not drain
6. Excessive vibration and noise
7. Washer fills but will not agitate
8. Washer agitates and spins (fast only)
9. Washer agitates and spins (slow only)
10. Washer will not spin
11. Timer will not advance
12. Washer will not spray rinse
13. Rinse water too hot
14. Rinse water too cold
15. Basket turns counter-clockwise during agitation
16. "Frozen" or damaged agitator
17. Cover shield loose, damaged, or off
18. Damaged washer body
19. Clothes retain lint
20. Odor in washer

●	Easy	No previous experience needed
● ●	Average	Requires removal of service panels. Mechanical ability is helpful.
● ● ●	Difficult	May require the use of an ohmmeter and/or splicing of electrical wires. Repair or replacement of component parts is more difficult.
● ● ● ●	Very difficult	May require the use of an ohmmeter and the ability to read a circuit diagram. Repair or replacement of component parts is complex.

No matter what skill level assigned to a task, study the repair procedure and safety instructions carefully before proceeding.

Problem diagnostic charts

Problem	Possible Cause	Repair Procedure	Skill Level
1. Washer will not operate	No power to washer	Check Power Supply (See p.17 & Procedure #1)	•
	Power cord or wiring defective	Check Power Cord (See p.19 & Procedure #2)	•••
		Check Wiring and Connections (See p.27 & Procedure #7)	•••
2. Washer will not fill	Blown fuse or tripped circuit breaker	Check Power Supply (See p.17 & Procedure #1)	•
	Water supply faucets closed	Check Faucets	•
	Clogged valve screens	Check Water Inlet Valve (See p.73 & Procedure #23)	•••
	Open valve solenoid	Check Water Inlet Valve (See p.73 & Procedure #23)	•••
	Water level switch defective	Check Water Level Switch (See p.31 & Procedure #9)	••••
		Check Wiring and Connections (See p.27 & Procedure #7)	•••
	Water temperature selector switch defective	Check Selector Switch (See p.29 & Procedure #8)	••••
		Check Wiring and Connections (See p.27 & Procedure #7)	•••
	Plastic housing timer defective	Check Plastic Housing Timer (See p.35 & Procedure #10)	••••
		(See p.39 & Procedure #11)	••••
		(See p.41 & Procedure #12)	••••
		(See p.47 & Procedure #13)	••••
		Check Wiring and Connections (See p.27 & Procedure #7)	•••
	Metal housing timer defective	Check Metal Housing Timer (See p.51 & Procedure #14)	••••
		(See p.53 & Procedure #15)	••••
		(see p.55 & Procedure #16)	••••
		Check Wiring and Connections (See p.27 & Procedure #7)	•••
	Kinked water hoses	Check Hoses (See p.73 & Procedure #23)	•••
		(See p.79 & Procedure #26)	•••

Skill Level Index: • **Easy** •• **Average** ••• **Difficult** •••• **Very Difficult**

Problem	Possible Cause	Repair Procedure	Skill Level
3. Washer will not stop filling	Water level switch defective	Check Water Level Switch (See p.31 & Procedure #9)	••••
	Foreign particles in inlet valve	Check Water Inlet Valve (See p.73 & Procedure #23)	•••
	Water inlet valve stuck open	Check Water Inlet Valve (See p.73 & Procedure #23)	•••
	Blockage in tube to water level switch	Check Water Level Switch (See p.31 & Procedure #9)	••••
	Leak in water level switch hose	Check Water Level Switch (See p.31 & Procedure #9)	••••
	Water level switch hose not vertical	Check Water Level Switch (See p.31 & Procedure #9)	••••
4. Washer leaking water on floor	Hose connections faulty or hose deteriorated	Check Water Inlet Valve (See p.73 & Procedure #23)	•••
		Check Pump (See p.79 & Procedure #26)	•••
	Drain hose improperly positioned or hose deteriorated	Check Pump (See p.79 & Procedure #26)	•••
	Cover gasket out of position or broken	Check Washer Cover (See p.23 & Procedure #4)	••
	Drainage pipe clogged	Check Pump (See p.79 & Procedure #26)	•••
	Spray out from plastic inlet	Check Water Inlet Valve (See p.73 & Procedure #23)	•••
	Splashing out of drain	Check *Use & Care Book*	
	Transmission boot defective	Check Transmission Boot (See p.65 & Procedure #20)	••••
		Check Agitator (See p.61 & Procedure #18)	••
	Tub or pump housing pitted	Check Pump (See p.79 & Procedure #26)	•••

Skill Level Index: • Easy •• Average ••• Difficult •••• Very Difficult

Problem	Possible Cause	Repair Procedure	Skill Level
5. **Washer will not drain**	Drain clogged	Check Pump (See p.79 & Procedure #26)	• • •
	Drain hose kinked or clogged	Check Pump (See p.79 & Procedure #26)	• • •
	Water pump defective	Check Pump (See p.79 & Procedure #26)	• • •
	Plastic housing timer defective (no spin)	Check Plastic Housing Timer (See p.35 & Procedure #10) (See p.39 & Procedure #11) (See p.41 & Procedure #12) (See p.47 & Procedure #13) Check Wiring and Connections (See p.27 & Procedure #7)	• • • • • • • • • • • • • • • • • • •
	Metal housing timer defective (no spin)	Check Metal Housing Timer (See p.51 & Procedure #14) (See p.53 & Procedure #15) (See p.55 & Procedure #16) Check Wiring and Connections (See p.27 & Procedure #7)	• • • • • • • • • • • • • • •
	Pump coupling defective	Check Pump Coupling (See p.77 & Procedure #25)	• • •
	Drain outlet too high	Check *Use & Care Book*	
6. **Excessive vibration and noise**	Machine not level	Check Leveling Legs (See p.26 & Procedure #6)	•
	Unbalanced load	Check *Use & Care Book*	
	Jam nuts missing or loose	Check Leveling Legs (See p.26 & Procedure #6)	•
	Floor weak or sloped	Check Leveling Legs (See p.26 & Procedure #6)	•
	Noisy transmission	Check Transmission (See p.69 & Procedure #21)	• • • •
	Clutch bearings worn	Check Single Speed Clutch (See p.81 & Procedure #27) Check Two-Speed Clutch (See p.85 & Procedure #28)	• • • • • • • •
	Clutch shoes worn	Check Single Speed Clutch (See p.81 & Procedure #27) Check Two-Speed Clutch (See p.85 & Procedure #28)	• • • • • • • •
	Motor shaft bent	Check Drive Motor (See p.93 & Procedure #30)	• • • •

Skill Level Index: • Easy • • Average • • • Difficult • • • • Very Difficult

Problem diagnostic charts (cont.)

Problem	Possible Cause	Repair Procedure	Skill Level
7. Washer fills but will not agitate	Transmission defective	Check Transmission (See p.69 & Procedure #21)	••••
		Check Agitator (See p.61 & Procedure #18)	••
	Plastic housing timer switch defective	Check Plastic Housing Timer	
		(See p.35 & Procedure #10)	••••
		(See p.39 & Procedure #11)	••••
		(See p.41 & Procedure #12)	••••
		(See p.47 & Procedure #13)	••••
		Check Wiring and Connections (See p.27 & Procedure #7)	•••
	Metal housing timer switch defective	Check Metal Housing Timer	
		(See p.51 & Procedure #14)	••••
		(See p.53 & Procedure #15)	••••
		(See p.55 & Procedure #16)	••••
		Check Wiring and Connections (See p.27 & Procedure #7)	•••
	Water level switch defective	Check Water Level Switch (See p.31 & Procedure #9)	••••
		Check Wiring and Connections (See p.27 & Procedure #7)	•••
	Drive motor defective	Check Drive Motor (See p.93 & Procedure #30)	••••
		Check Wiring and Connections (See p.27 & Procedure #7)	•••
	Motor start relay defective	Check Motor Start Relay (See p.71 & Procedure #22)	••••
		Check Wiring and Connections (See p.27 & Procedure #7)	•••
	Open motor protector	Check Drive Motor (See p.93 & Procedure #30)	••••
		Check Wiring and Connections (See p.27 & Procedure #7)	•••
	Lid switch defective	Check Lid Switch (See p.63 & Procedure #19)	•••
		Check Wiring and Connections (See p.27 & Procedure #7)	•••
	Loose or broken drive belt	Check Belt (See p.75 & Procedure #24)	•••

Skill Level Index: • Easy •• Average ••• Difficult •••• Very Difficult

Problem	Possible Cause	Repair Procedure	Skill Level
8. Washer agitates and spins (fast only)	Speed shifter or solenoid defective	Check Two-Speed Clutch Shifter (See p.91 & Procedure #29)	••••
		Check Wiring and Connections (See p.27 & Procedure #7)	•••
	Speed shifter needs adjustment	Check Two-Speed Clutch Shifter (See p.91 & Procedure #29)	••••
	Lower carrier plate defective	Check Two-Speed Clutch (See p.85 & Procedure #28)	••••
	Plastic housing timer defective (some models)	Check Plastic Housing Timer (See p.35 & Procedure #10)	••••
		(See p.39 & Procedure #11)	••••
		(See p.41 & Procedure #12)	••••
		(See p.47 & Procedure #13)	••••
		Check Wiring and Connections (See p.27 & Procedure #7)	•••
	Metal housing timer defective (some models)	Check Metal Housing Timer (See p.51 & Procedure #14)	••••
		(See p.53 & Procedure #15)	••••
		(See p.55 & Procedure #16)	••••
		Check Wiring and Connections (See p.27 & Procedure #7)	•••
	Selector switch defective	Check Selector Switch (See p.29 & Procedure #8)	••••
		Check Wiring and Connections (See p.27 & Procedure #7)	•••
9. Washer agitates and spins (slow only)	Shifter bent	Check Two-Speed Clutch Shifter (See p.91 & Procedure #29)	••••
	Lower carrier plate binding	Check Two-Speed Clutch (See p.85 & Procedure #28)	••••

Skill Level Index: • Easy •• Average ••• Difficult •••• Very Difficult

Problem diagnostic charts (cont.)

Problem	Possible Cause	Repair Procedure	Skill Level
10. **Washer will not spin**	Plastic housing timer switch defective	Check Plastic Housing Timer	
		(See p.35 & Procedure #10)	• • • •
		(See p.39 & Procedure #11)	• • • •
		(See p.41 & Procedure #12)	• • • •
		(See p.47 & Procedure #13)	• • • •
		Check Wiring and Connections	
		(See p.27 & Procedure #7)	• • •
	Metal housing timer switch defective	Check Metal Housing Timer	
		(See p.51 & Procedure #14)	• • • •
		(See p.53 & Procedure #15)	• • • •
		(See p.55 & Procedure #16)	• • • •
		Check Wiring and Connections	
		(See p.27 & Procedure #7)	• • •
	Drive motor defective	Check Drive Motor	
		(See p.93 & Procedure #30)	• • • •
		Check Wiring and Connections	
		(See p.27 & Procedure #7)	• • •
	Lid switch defective	Check Lid Switch	
		(See p.63 & Procedure #19)	• • •
		Check Wiring and Connections	
		(See p.27 & Procedure #7)	• • •
	Motor start relay defective	Check Motor Start Relay	
		(See p.71 & Procedure #22)	• • • •
		Check Wiring and Connections	
		(See p.27 & Procedure #7)	• • •
	Open motor protector	Check Drive Motor	
		(See p.93 & Procedure #30)	• • • •
		Check Wiring and Connections	
		(See p.27 & Procedure #7)	• • •
	Transmission defective	Check Transmission	
		(See p.69 & Procedure #21)	• • • •
	Loose or broken drive belt	Check Belt	
		(See p.75 & Procedure #24)	• • •
	Blown fuse or tripped circuit breaker	Check Power Supply	
		(See p.17 & Procedure #1)	•

Skill Level Index: • Easy • • Average • • • Difficult • • • • Very Difficult

Problem	Possible Cause	Repair Procedure	Skill Level
11. **Timer will not advance**	Open plastic housing timer motor	Check Plastic Housing Timer (See p.35 & Procedure #10) (See p.39 & Procedure #11) (See p.41 & Procedure #12) (See p.47 & Procedure #13) Check Wiring and Connections (See p.27 & Procedure #7)	• • • • • • • • • • • • • • • • • • •
	Open metal housing timer motor	Check Metal Housing Timer (See p.51 & Procedure #14) (See p.53 & Procedure #15) (See p.55 & Procedure #16) Check Wiring and Connections (See p.27 & Procedure #7)	• • • • • • • • • • • • • • •
12. **Washer will not spray rinse**	Drain system restricted	Check Pump (See p.79 & Procedure #26)	• • •
	Plastic housing timer defective	Check Plastic Housing Timer (See p.35 & Procedure #10) (See p.39 & Procedure #11) (See p.41 & Procedure #12) (See p.47 & Procedure #13) Check Wiring and Connections (See p.27 & Procedure #7)	• • • • • • • • • • • • • • • • • • •
	Metal housing timer defective	Check Metal Housing Timer (See p.51 & Procedure #14) (See p.53 & Procedure #15) (See p.55 & Procedure #16) Check Wiring and Connections (See p.27 & Procedure #7)	• • • • • • • • • • • • • • •
	Water level switch not resetting	Check Water Level Switch (See p.31 & Procedure #9) Check Wiring and Connections (See p.27 & Procedure #7)	• • • • • • •
13. **Rinse water too hot**	Faucets misadjusted	Check *Use & Care Book*	
	Hoses reversed at inlet valve or supply faucets	Check Water Inlet Valve (See p.73 & Procedure #23) Check Wiring and Connections (See p.27 & Procedure #7)	• • • • • •
	Wires reversed at inlet valve	Check Water Inlet Valve (See p.73 & Procedure #23) Check Wiring and Connections (See p.27 & Procedure #7)	• • • • • •

Skill Level Index: • Easy •• Average ••• Difficult •••• Very Difficult

Problem diagnostic charts (cont.)

Problem	Possible Cause	Repair Procedure	Skill Level
14. **Rinse water too cold**	Faucets misadjusted	Check *Use & Care Book*	
	Hot water supply exhausted	Check *Use & Care Book*	
	Dirt, corrosion, sand, or lime deposits around inlet valve	Check Water Inlet Valve (See p.73 & Procedure #23)	●●●
15. **Basket turns counter-clockwise during agitation**	Transmission defective	Check Transmission (See p.69 & Procedure #21) Check Agitator (See p.61 & Procedure #18)	●●●● ●●
16. **"Frozen" or damaged agitator**	Agitator defective	Check Agitator (See p.61 & Procedure #18)	●●
17. **Cover shield loose, damaged, or off**	Cover shield defective	Check Cover Shield (See p.59 & Procedure #17)	●●
18. **Damaged washer body**	Scratches, dents, rust or discoloration	Check Cosmetics (See p.95 & Procedure #31)	●
19. **Clothes retain lint**	Lint-holding fabrics washed with lint-giving fabrics	Check *Use & Care Book*	
	Clothes load too small for water level	Check *Use & Care Book*	
	Tub outlet blocked	Check Pump (See p.79 & Procedure #26)	●●●
	Pump inoperative	Check Pump (See p.79 & Procedure #26)	●●●
20. **Odor in washer**	Accumulated lint or deposit on washtub	Remove lint and deposits See Preventive Maintenance	
	Unusually dirty washload	See Preventive Maintenance	
	Accumulated lint or deposit around agitator	Check Agitator (See p.61 & Procedure #18)	●●

Skill Level Index: ● **Easy** ●● **Average** ●●● **Difficult** ●●●● **Very Difficult**

Repair procedures

How to use the repair procedures

The following washer repair procedures take you step-by-step through repairs for most of the washer problems you are likely to encounter. The Problem Diagnostic Charts on pages 7-15 will help you to pinpoint the likely causes of your problem. Beginning with the most likely cause, you can then refer to the appropriate repair procedure section.

Each repair procedure is a complete inspection and repair process for a single washer component, containing the information you need to test a component that may be faulty and to replace it, if necessary. This format breaks down even some of the most complex repair problems into separate, easy-to-handle units. Following the instructions given, you can test each component separately, isolating the cause of the problem and replacing any faulty parts. If one procedure fails to locate the failed component, you simply refer back to the Problem Diagnostic Charts for the next most likely cause of the problem.

Featuring a close-up photograph of the component you will be testing, the repair procedure begins with a description of what the component does and how it works. In the case of a component which varies with different washer models, you will be shown how to determine which type is found on your washer.

Instructions showing how to test and replace the component begin with steps that must be followed to assure your safety. Other initial steps indicate the skills and equipment that will be needed for the task. If you are uncertain about a process that will be used, such as reading a circuit diagram, using an ohmmeter, or removing access panels, you are referred to the pages in this manual where that process is discussed in detail. No matter what your skill level, careful attention must be paid to these instructions and safety precautions before you begin any procedure.

Clear photographs of typical washer models illustrate each step of every repair procedure, proceeding from visual inspection and testing to replacement of the component. Because of the diversity of washer models available, your washer may differ somewhat from the illustrated model. However, each procedure has been carefully designed to be representative of the entire General Electric and Hotpoint lines, and as much information as possible has been included to help you make repairs on most General Electric and Hotpoint washers.

NOTE:
The repair procedures are listed below in the order in which they appear in this section. Refer to the Problem Diagnostic Charts on pages 7-15 for the procedure most likely to remedy your problem, then use this list to locate the desired procedure.

Washer repair procedures

1. Circuit Breakers and Fuses
2. Power Cord
3. Operating Panel
4. Washer Cover
5. Rear Access Panel
6. Leveling Legs
7. Wiring and Connections
8. Selector Switches
9. Water Level Switches
10. Inspecting Plastic Housing Timer Switches
11. Replacing Plastic Housing Timer Switches #1 and #3
12. Disassembling Plastic Housing Timer
13. Plastic Housing Timer Hub
14. Inspecting Metal Housing Timer Switches and Motor
15. Replacing Metal Housing Timer Switches and Motor
16. Disassembling Metal Housing Timer
17. Cover Shield
18. Agitator
19. Lid Switch
20. Transmission Boot
21. Transmission
22. Motor Start Relay
23. Water Inlet Valve
24. Belt
25. Pump Coupling
26. Pump
27. Single Speed Clutch
28. Two-Speed Clutch
29. Two-Speed Clutch Shifter
30. Drive Motor
31. Cosmetic Repairs

1 Inspecting circuit breakers and fuses

Skill Level Rating:	Easy	Average	Difficult	Very Difficult

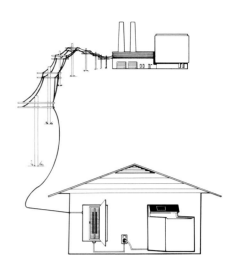

Electricity produced by the power company is delivered to your house through a series of connecting power lines. A power supply distribution panel is located at the point where the main line from the power company enters your home. One of two types of distribution panels services your household; either a circuit breaker panel or a fuse panel. From the distribution panel the power line is divided into a number of smaller circuits that are distributed to various household appliances, receptacles, and lights. Each of these circuits is protected from becoming overloaded by either a circuit breaker or fuse.

It's important to know which breakers or fuses protect each circuit in your home. It's also wise to label them when everything is operating correctly, so that you'll know which breaker or fuse to look for in time of trouble.

The distribution panel is the place to turn off all power on the washer circuit before unplugging and servicing it. And it's the first place to look when problems occur. A tripped circuit breaker or blown fuse is a minor problem, but it can stop the entire washer from working.

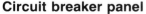

Circuit breaker panel

Fuse panel

1 continued

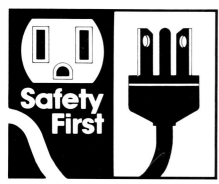

Step 1: Be sure all washer controls are turned **OFF**. Avoid touching any grounded objects such as water pipes when working around power supply. Stand on a dry insulated surface such as a dry board.

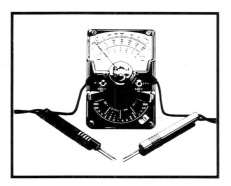

Step 2: This procedure requires the use of an ohmmeter. For instructions on how to use an ohmmeter, please refer to Tools and Testing Equipment, page 101.

Step 3: Other than opening the door to the distribution panel, never remove any cover or expose any electrical terminals.

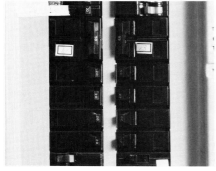

Step 4: Circuit breakers. Circuit breaker distribution panels contain rows of switches. When a breaker "trips", power is shut off and the breaker switch moves to an intermediate position between the "ON" and "OFF" points.

Step 5: To restore power, turn the breaker switch to "OFF" position, then back to "ON". If the breaker trips again, the circuit is still overloaded. Further exploration of the problem is necessary before power supply can be restored.

Step 6: Fuses. A second type of distribution panel is protected by fuses. To restore power when a fuse "blows", it is necessary to replace the old fuse with a new one of the same amperage.

Step 7: Fuses for your washer can simply be screwed in or out by hand. If new fuse blows, circuit may still be overloaded or short circuited and further investigation is needed before power can be restored.

Step 8: Faulty or blown fuses cannot always be discovered simply by looking. Some will be obviously blown while others may have only invisible changes within that can interrupt the flow of current.

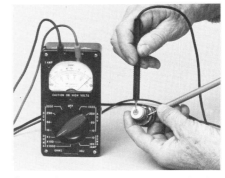

Step 9: Fuses may be checked with ohmmeter. Set ohmmeter to R x 1. Touch one test probe to brass tip and other probe to shell at base of fuse. If test shows no continuity, replace fuse.

2 Inspecting and replacing power cord

Skill Level Rating:	Easy	Average	**Difficult**	Very Difficult

Your General Electric or Hotpoint washer has a special power cord which carries current from a three-prong grounded outlet to the appliance. If the washer fails to operate, the power cord may be preventing power from reaching the washer. Most power cord problems are caused by damaged or loose connections that will likely be visible.

Power cord

Washer plug

Step 1: For your personal safety, exercise caution when working with any electrical appliance.

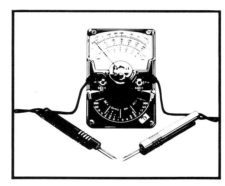

Step 2: This procedure requires the use of an ohmmeter. For instructions on how to use an ohmmeter, please refer to Tools and Testing Equipment, page 101.

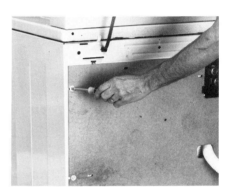

Step 3: This procedure requires removal of rear access panel from your washer. If you are unfamiliar with this process, refer to Procedure #5: Removing Rear Access Panel.

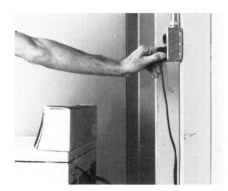

Step 4: Protect floor covering. Pull washer away from wall, making power cord completely visible. Pull plug from receptacle with firm, quick tug. Always grasp by plug and never by cord to prevent cord damage. Be careful not to contact blades of plug with fingers.

Step 5: Inspect plug for damaged, corroded, or burned prongs. A damaged plug may indicate poor connections inside wall receptacle. If so, have receptacle checked by a qualified electrician. If plug is damaged, replace the cord as described in Steps 13-14.

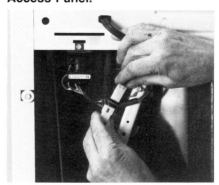

Step 6: Pull apart two halves of power cord disconnect and visually inspect them. If disconnect is cracked or burned, it should be replaced.

19

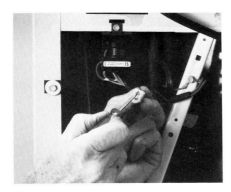

Step 7: To replace disconnect, depress locking tabs on terminals with tweezers or small screwdriver and push them out. Snap new disconnect into place.

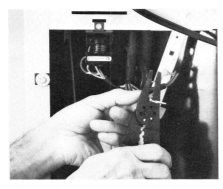

Step 8: To replace a single damaged terminal, cut damaged terminal off and follow steps 9 and 10 for wire stripping and crimping.

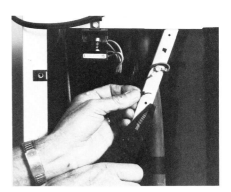

Step 9: If the power cord wire is broken near terminal, cut cord at break. Strip off ¼ inch of insulation.

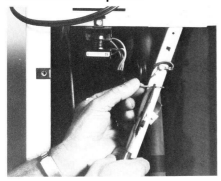

Step 10: Using a crimping tool, crimp on new terminal and snap into block.

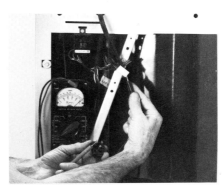

Step 11: If no visible damage to power cord is detected, ohmmeter must be used to check for defective wires. Set ohmmeter to R x 1. Touch one probe to one prong on power cord plug and second probe to either pin on other end of cord.

Step 12: Follow above procedure for other pin and grounding wire screw, twisting cord each time with ohmmeter probes in place to check for internal breakage. Repeat same procedure for other two prongs on power cord plug. Replace cord if continuity is not found on all checks.

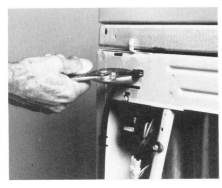

Step 13: To remove power cord from washer, squeeze strain relief with pliers as shown to remove it from cabinet. Pull power cord out through opening.

Step 14: Replace power cord. Insert strain relief with pliers and press in. Be sure all wiring connections are secure. Reassemble washer and reconnect power supply.

3 Removing operating panel

Skill Level Rating:	Easy	Average	Difficult	Very Difficult

The operating panel is mounted to the front of the backsplash assembly. All the manually operated switches and controls are located on it. It is one of three removable access panels on your washer. Inside it are the selector switches, the timer, and the water level switch.

There are two styles of backsplashes--one 6 inches high and one 7 inches high. Methods for the removal of the operating panels differ slightly. Steps 2 through 4 describe removal of the operating panel from the 6-inch backsplash. Steps 5 through 9 cover the 7-inch backsplash.

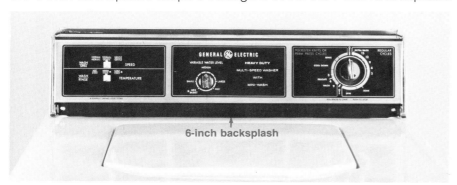

6-inch backsplash

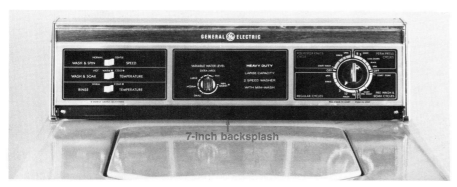

7-inch backsplash

3 continued

Step 1: Be sure all washer controls are turned **OFF**. Unplug the washer from the receptacle. Watch for sharp edges.

Step 2: Removing 6 inch operating panel. Using Phillips screwdriver, remove two screws from top.

Step 3: Remove two bottom front screws.

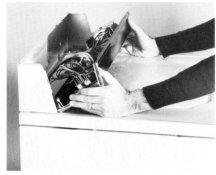

Step 4: Roll top of operating panel toward front of the washer. This exposes timer and switches.

Step 5: Removing 7 inch operating panel. Using a Phillips screwdriver, remove two top screws.

Step 6: Lift rear of top trim and roll toward front of the washer.

Step 7: Remove two Phillips screws from bottom front.

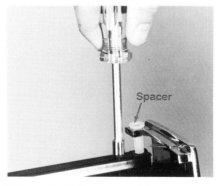

Spacer

Step 8: Using a nutdriver, remove two hex head screws and spacers from top.

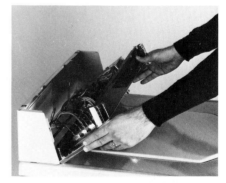

Step 9: Roll top of operating panel toward front of washer. This provides access to timer and switches. Reassemble washer and reconnect power supply.

4 Opening washer cover

Skill Level Rating:	Easy	**Average**	Difficult	Very Difficult

The cover is attached to the washer cabinet (or apron) by four spring clips. For access to the interior of the washer, the cover can be raised. On almost all General Electric models, first raise the lid and detach the Filter Flo® nozzle from the white plastic cover shield. On Dispensall™ models, the plastic separator tabs (see illustration) must be detached from the cover shield first. Otherwise, raising the cover might break the molded pin on the diverter located at the tub wall.

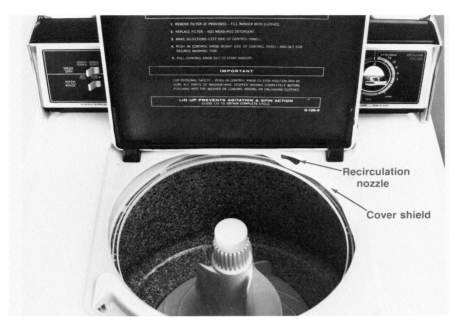

Filter-Flo® model

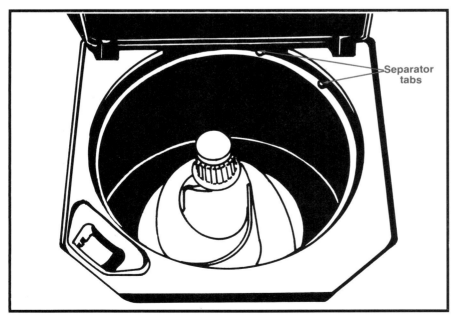

Dispensall™ model

4 continued

Step 1: Be sure all washer controls are turned **OFF**. Unplug the washer from the receptacle. Watch for sharp edges.

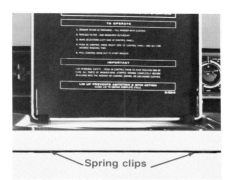

Spring clips

Step 2: The washer cover is attached by two spring clips at the front and two clips at the rear. The location of the front spring clips can be pinpointed by observing the front washer panel at eye level.

Step 3: Using a one inch putty knife, push in on the front spring clips. Note: Do not use a large-bladed screwdriver. It may chip the cover.

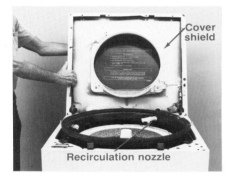

Cover shield

Recirculation nozzle

Step 4: Tip cover back while supporting lid. Lean against wall or hold to avoid stressing electrical connection. Do not disengage rear spring slips. Note: On General Electric models, disengage recirculation nozzle or diverter from cover shield.

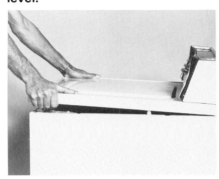

Step 5: To replace the cover, hook the rear flange over the two rear cover spring clips and press down until the front clips snap into place.

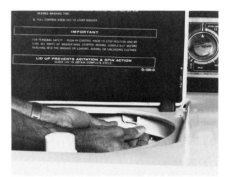

Step 6: Pull the recirculation nozzle back through the cover shield. Reconnect power supply.

5 Removing rear access panel

Skill Level Rating: | **Easy** | Average | Difficult | Very Difficult |

The rear access panel, or apron back, is a fiber board held in place by 5/16″ hex head screws. It's a safety device which protects electrical components and moving parts and also helps to reduce vibration and sound level.

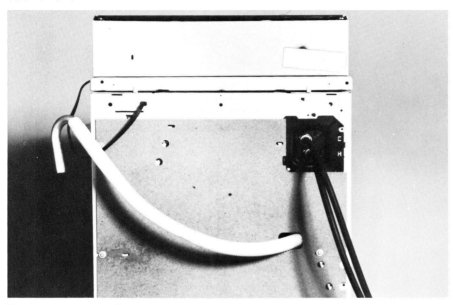

Rear access panel

Step 1: Be sure all washer controls are turned **OFF**. Unplug the washer from the receptacle. Watch for sharp edges on access panels.

Step 2: Using a nutdriver, loosen screws on left side and remove screws on right side.

Step 3: Slide panel to right and remove it.

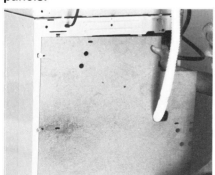

Step 4: To replace rear access panel, slip it under three screws on left side. Replace all other screws. Tighten all screws. Reconnect power supply.

6 Adjusting leveling legs

Skill Level Rating:	Easy	Average	Difficult	Very Difficult

Your washer has four leveling legs. The rear two are self-adjusting and adapt to the floor, while the front two can be adjusted to provide your washer with maximum stability so that it rests solidly and firmly on the floor.

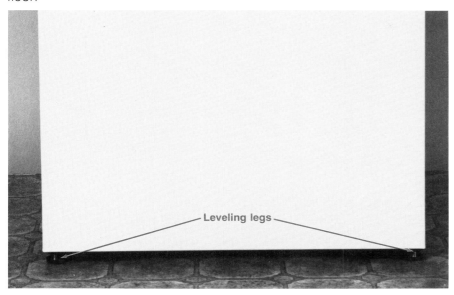

Leveling legs

Leveling legs

Step 1: For your personal safety, exercise caution when working with any electrical appliance.

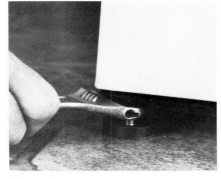

Step 2: To adjust front leveling legs, loosen jam nuts which hold legs to bottom of washer.

Step 3: Adjust front legs so that the washer rests solidly on floor. Tighten jam nuts against washer base.

Step 4: With hands on washer cover, rock washer to be sure it rests solidly on the floor. Be sure four rubber leveling pads are all in place.

26

7 Repairing wiring and connections

| Skill Level Rating: | Easy | Average | **Difficult** | Very Difficult |

Electrical current is carried to the components of your washer by a network of color-coded, heat-resistant wires. These wires are connected to various switches and heating systems primarily by push-on terminals; spliced wires are protected with a molded rubber covering or with connectors.

Wires connected to terminals are susceptible to damage from arcing and heat build-up. If terminals are dull and oxidized (rusty-looking), they should be replaced. Any mating terminal, such as one located on a switch or disconnect terminal, should be polished until bright and shiny before a new wire is attached. This practice assures a good connection.

When checking electrical connections, you may need to follow the circuit diagram that is located either on the back of the washer or inside the backsplash.

Note: If replacement wire is required, use only appliance wire having the same temperature and gauge rating as the wire you are replacing.

Note: For installation reference, make note of how wires are connected. Use masking tape to mark wires or draw a diagram on paper.

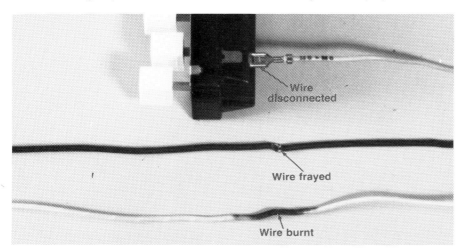

Typical wiring problems encountered

Step 1: Be sure all washer controls are turned **OFF**. Unplug the washer from the receptacle. Watch for sharp edges on access panels and parts.

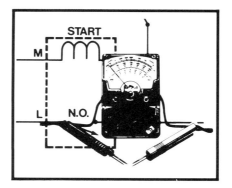

Step 2: This procedure requires the use of an ohmmeter and the ability to read a circuit diagram. For instructions, refer to Tools and Testing Equipment, pages 101-104.

Step 3: Most washer electrical connections are accessed by removing operating panel or washer cover. If you are unfamiliar with this process, refer to Procedure #3: Removing Operating Panel or Procedure #4 Opening Washer Cover.

7 continued

Step 4: Push-on male/female connections are typical of those used in washer applications. Repairs may be necessary to either terminal or wire. Be sure these terminals fit together snugly to make a solid connection.

Step 5: Wires are color coded. Follow wires on circuit diagram located inside operating panel or on rear access panel for connection information.

Step 6: When removing push-on connectors from terminals, label wires with tape or make a sketch of connections to assure proper installation when reassembling washer.

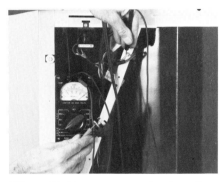

Step 7: To test a particular wire, disconnect one end from male terminal connection, and place ohmmeter probes across both ends of wire. You should observe continuity on R x 1 scale.

Step 8: If no continuity (needle does not move), check area where wire is attached to female terminal. If attachment is solid, replace wire.

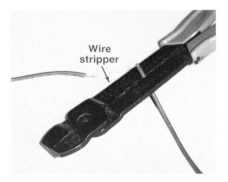

Step 9: To splice, cut wire using wire strippers. When stripping insulation, remove only enough insulation to make splice, being careful not to cut wire. Usually 5/8" is sufficient.

Step 10: Washer wiring should be spliced only by using a wire nut or bell connector. After stripping insulation back to bright and shiny wire, twist wires together and secure with wire nut.

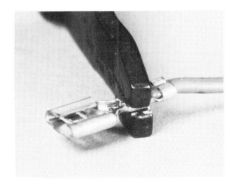

Step 11: Should terminal need replacing, cut old terminal from wire. Strip wire end and twist strands together. Slip new terminal over twisted wire strands and crimp terminal down over them securely with a terminal crimping tool.

Step 12: After making any necessary repairs, reassemble washer and reconnect power supply.

8 Inspecting and replacing selector switches

Skill Level Rating:	Easy	Average	Difficult	**Very Difficult**

The selector switches are located in the backsplash and are fastened to the back side of the operating panel with hex head screws. Externally, depending on your washer, these switches may be toggle, rotary, or pushbutton, but they all perform basically the same functions.

The selector switches control: water temperature, agitation rate, spin speed, and optional features like extra rinse and suds save/return.

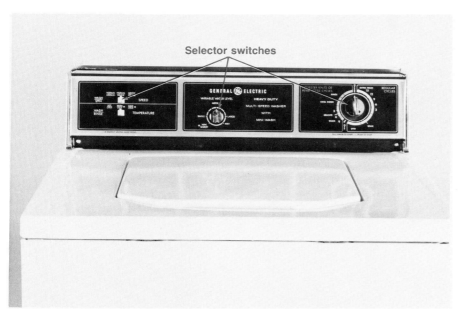

Selector switches

Step 1: Be sure all washer controls are turned **OFF**. Unplug the washer from the receptacle. Watch for sharp edges on operating panel and parts.

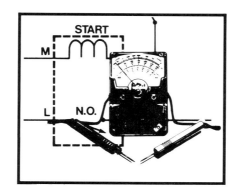

Step 2: This procedure requires the use of an ohmmeter and the ability to read a circuit diagram. For instructions, refer to Tools and Testing Equipment, pages 101-104.

Step 3: Remove your washer's operating panel. If you are unfamiliar with this process, refer to Procedure #3: Removing Operating Panel.

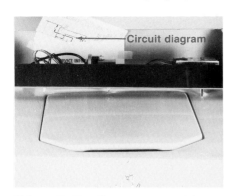

Step 4: To diagnose a problem with your washer's selector switch, refer to your circuit diagram and cam chart.

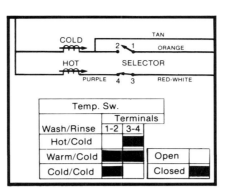

Step 5: On the bottom of your circuit diagram, locate the chart for the selector switches and determine whether the switches should be open or closed.

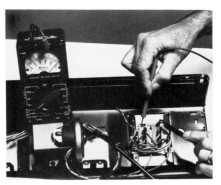

Step 6: Set ohmmeter for R x 1. With at least one wire detached, apply ohmmeter probes to switch terminals labeled "CLOSED" on chart. Replace switch if there is no continuity. Check all pairs of contacts for all switch knob positions.

Step 7: For installation reference, make note of how wires are connected by labeling wires. Remove wires.

Step 8: With a nutdriver, remove hex screws which fasten selector switch to inside of operating panel.

Step 9: Carefully remove entire selector switch from operating panel. (For rotary switches remove knob first).

Step 10: Replace with a new selector switch.

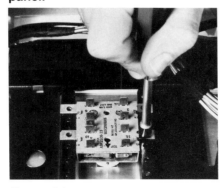

Step 11: Replace hex screws in new selector switch with nutdriver.

Step 12: Carefully replace wires. (Replace knob on rotary switch). Reassemble washer and reconnect power supply.

9 Inspecting and replacing water level switches

Skill Level Rating:	Easy	Average	Difficult	**Very Difficult**

A major backsplash component is the water level switch, or pressure switch. It controls the amount of water entering the washer. Water level selection may include: SMALL, MEDIUM, LARGE, and EXTRA LARGE. Special features are also available such as MINI-WASH® wash system (GE) and HANDWASH® control system (Hotpoint). Most of these switches will be either a toggle or a rotary switch. Some models have a fixed water level switch for which there is no adjustment.

Note: If the machine is not empty of water, set the selector switch to spin it out and drain the washer until the water level in the machine is at least below the bottom of the wash basket.

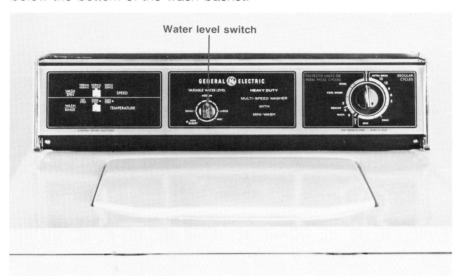

Water level switch

Water level switch

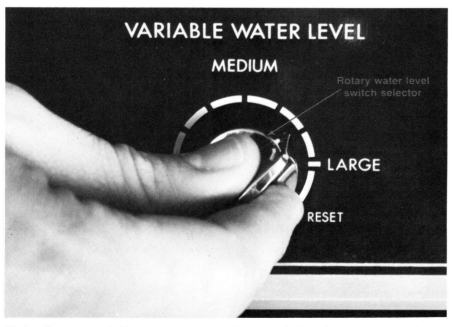

Note: If your model has a rotary water level switch selector, remove knob from front of operating panel by pulling it off.

31

9 continued

Step 1: Be sure all washer controls are turned **OFF**. Unplug the washer from the receptacle. Watch for sharp edges on operating panel and parts.

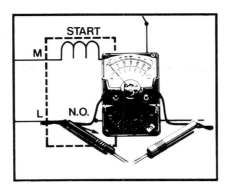

Step 2: This procedure requires the use of an ohmmeter and the ability to read a circuit diagram and cam chart. For instructions, refer to Tools and Testing Equipment, pages 101-104.

Step 3: Remove your washer's operating panel. If you are unfamiliar with this process, refer to Procedure #3: Removing Operating Panel.

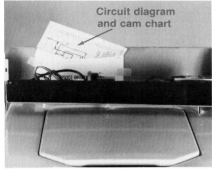

Step 4: To diagnose a problem with your washer's water level switch, refer to your circuit diagram and cam chart.

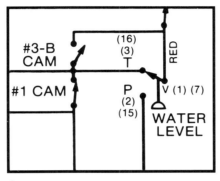

Step 5: Locate the water level switch terminals which are labeled on the circuit diagram for your washer. The terminal identification may vary with different groups of numbers or letters, but the function is the same.

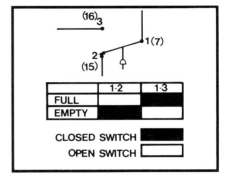

Step 6: On the sample diagram, the contacts should be open or closed as shown in this chart. With both of their wires disconnected, terminals 2 and 3 should never show any continuity.

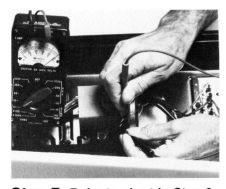

Step 7: Refer to chart in Step 6 to see whether comparable terminals on switch should be open or closed. Test appropriate contacts for continuity with ohmmeter. Needle should sweep upscale to 0 when switch is closed; if not, replace switch.

Step 8: If your model has a rotary water level switch selector, remove knob from front of operating panel by pulling it off.

Step 9: Remove water level switch hose from switch.

9 continued

Step 10: For installation reference, make note of how wires are connected by labeling the wires.

Step 11: With a nutdriver, remove hex screws which fasten water level switch to inside of operating panel.

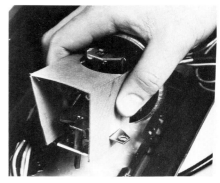

Step 12: Carefully remove water level switch from operating panel.

Step 13: Replace with a new water level switch.

Step 14: Replace hex screws in new water level switch with nutdriver. Be sure hose is replaced and secured.

Step 15: Carefully reattach wires.

Step 16: Replace operating panel and control knob. Reconnect power supply.

Step 17: Set control knob for spin cycle, and spin for at least one minute. Check water level switch by setting at desired level and allowing washer to fill. Check water level.

Notes

10 Inspecting plastic housing timer switches

Skill Level Rating: | Easy | Average | Difficult | **Very Difficult** |

The timer, located in the backsplash behind the control knob, is the brain of your washer. It tells the other components when to start and stop and how long to run. There are two different types of timers used in General Electric and Hotpoint washers. Your washer will have either a metal housing timer or a plastic housing timer. If your timer's outside case or "housing" is metal, refer to Procedures #14-16.

The plastic housing timer parts work together to control the operation of your washer's cycles. The molded switches numbered 1 through 4 each have a special function. To fully understand what each switch controls, refer to your circuit diagram and cam chart or your wiring label. Find each switch on both the diagram and the chart to determine the function of each switch.

The #1 switch controls the whole drive motor circuit. It turns the drive motor on and off. The #3 switch has a dual function. The two lower terminals are the main power switch, and the middle and upper terminals provide a bypass around the water level switch during the spin function. Switches #1 and #3 can be replaced without disassembling the entire timer.

Switch #2 controls any special functions your washer has, and #4 reverses the direction of the drive motor to provide both agitation and spin (modes A and B). The printed circuit switches control the water valve solenoids. Between switches #3 and #2 is the PUSH-PULL switch which you control through the knob on your operating panel when you select your cycle.

When you set the controls for a particular cycle, the motor and gears drive the circular cam at a certain speed, and the cam followers activate the switch contacts to give the correct sequence of events.

Note: Procedures #10, #11, #12, and #13 all deal with the plastic housing timer. Timer procedures follow this sequence:
Procedure #10: Inspecting Plastic Housing Timer Switches
Procedure #11: Replacing Plastic Housing Timer Switches #1 and #3
Procedure #12: Disassembling Plastic Housing Timer
Procedure #13: Inspecting and Replacing Plastic Timer Hub

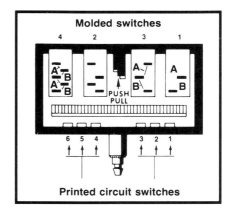

Timer switches

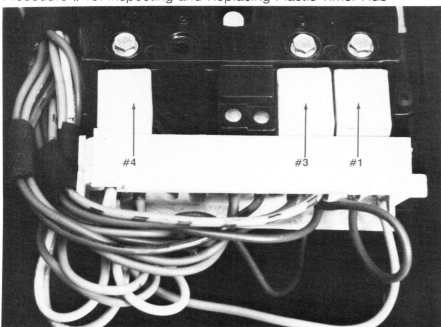

Plastic housing timer switches

35

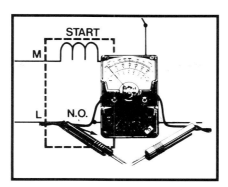

Step 1: Be sure all washer controls including timer are turned **OFF**. Unplug washer from receptacle. Watch for sharp edges on parts.

Step 2: This procedure requires the use of an ohmmeter and the ability to read a circuit diagram. For instructions, refer to Tools and Testing Equipment, pages 101-104.

Step 3: This procedure requires removal of operating panel from your washer. If you are not familiar with this process, refer to Procedure #3: Removing Operating Panel.

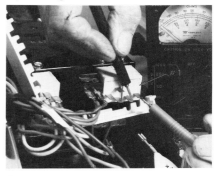

Step 4: Open switch cover by freeing plastic tab, lifting top part and laying it back. For installation reference, make note of how wires are connected.

Step 5: Remove wires from switch to be checked.

Step 6: Set ohmmeter for R x 1. With timer set at "OFF", use ohmmeter to check switches #1, #3A, and #3B individually. When timer is at "OFF", these switches should be open. Circuit should not have continuity.

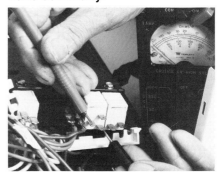

Step 7: To test switches #4A and #4B with ohmmeter, timer should be set at "OFF". Be sure to refer to your cam chart to determine whether switch #4 should be open or closed with timer at "OFF".

Step 8: Set timer for beginning of agitation function in WASH cycle. When you test switches #1, #3A and both pairs of #4A contacts with ohmmeter, they should be closed, or have continuity. Needle should sweep upscale to 0.

Step 9: With timer still set for WASH, test switches #3B and #4B with ohmmeter. They should be open, or have no continuity. Needle will remain downscale. Be sure to check both pairs of #4B contacts.

10 continued

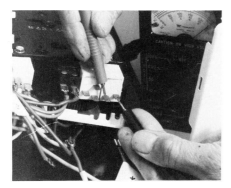

Step 10: Set timer to SPIN. With ohmmeter, test switches #1, #3A, #3B, and both #4B contacts. They should be closed, showing continuity, with needle sweeping to 0.

Step 11: With timer set to SPIN, test both pairs of contacts for switch #4A. They should be open, or show no continuity. Needle should not move.

Step 12: If your timer has a switch #2, refer to cam chart to determine when switch should be open or closed during the cycle. Rotate timer dial through cycle with ohmmeter connected to see if it registers open and closed at appropriate times.

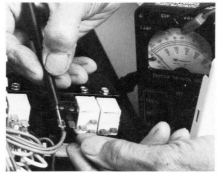

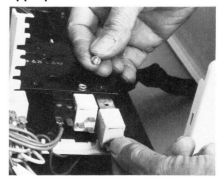

Step 13: Test timer motor winding for continuity with ohmmeter set at R x 100 by removing at least one wire. Touch ohmmeter probes to both terminals. The needle should sweep.

Step 14: Test PUSH-PULL switch with ohmmeter by removing at least one wire. With knob pushed in, switch should be open, having no continuity. With knob out, switch should be closed, showing that circuit has continuity.

Step 15: If switches #1 and #3 are faulty, following Procedure #11: Replacing Plastic Housing Timer Switches #1 and #3. All other switches can only be replaced by disassembling the timer. (See Procedure #12: Disassembling Plastic Housing Timer).

Notes

11 Replacing plastic housing timer switches #1 and #3

Skill Level Rating: | Easy | Average | Difficult | **Very Difficult** |

Switches #1 and #3 in the plastic housing timer can be replaced without disassembling the timer or removing it from the backsplash. To determine if this is necessary, read carefully Procedure #10: Inspecting Plastic Housing Timer Switches. Follow the instructions for testing switches after familiarizing yourself with the function and location of each switch. If switch #1 or #3 is faulty, remove and replace it.

Note: Procedures #10, #11, #12, and #13 all deal with the plastic housing timer. Timer procedures follow this sequence:
Procedure #10: Inspecting Plastic Housing Timer Switches
Procedure #11: Replacing Plastic Housing Timer Switches #1 and #3
Procedure #12: Disassembling Plastic Housing Timer
Procedure #13: Inspecting and Replacing Plastic Housing Timer Hub

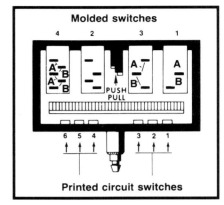

Timer switches

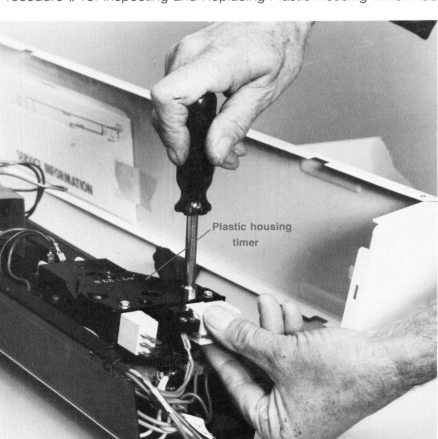

Removing plastic housing timer switch #3

11 continued

Step 1: Be sure all washer controls including timer are turned **OFF**. Unplug washer from receptacle. Watch for sharp edges.

Step 2: Set timer in "OFF" position. Remove hex-head screws holding switches (#1 and/or #3) in place. Note: If #1 switch is replaced, also check #4 switch.

Step 3: Gently work switch out of timer. Inspect switch for burned contacts.

Step 4: Replace switch by slipping new one into place.

Step 5: Use nutdriver to replace the ¼" mounting screws in new switch.

Step 6: Reassemble washer and reconnect power supply.

12 Disassembling plastic housing timer

Skill Level Rating: | Easy | Average | Difficult | **Very Difficult** |

Before considering completely disassembling the plastic housing timer, read Procedure #10: Inspecting Plastic Housing Timer Switches. After familiarizing yourself with the parts of your timer and their functions, carefully test all the switches, using an ohmmeter. If the problem is in switch #1 or #3, these two can be easily replaced without removing the timer from the backsplash (see Procedure #11: Replacing Plastic Housing Timer Swtiches #1 and #3). Any other problem will entail complete disassembly of the timer.

Note: Before beginning Procedure #12: Disassembling Plastic Housing Timer, be sure you familiarize yourself with the various timer parts.

Note: Procedures #10, #11, #12, and #13 all deal with the plastic housing timer. Timer procedures follow this sequence:
Procedure #10: Inspecting Plastic Housing Timer Switches
Procedure #11: Replacing Plastic Housing Timer Switches #1 and #3
Procedure #12: Disassembling Plastic Housing Timer
Procedure #13: Inspecting and Replacing Plastic Housing Timer Hub

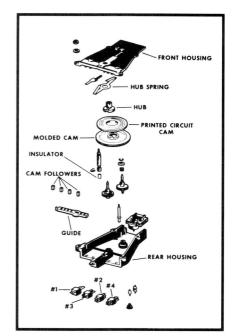

Plastic housing timer (exploded view)

Plastic housing timer

12 continued

Step 1: Be sure all washer controls including timer are turned **OFF**. Unplug washer from receptacle. Watch for sharp edges on parts.

Step 2: Remove three hex-head screws which hold timer to inside of backsplash.

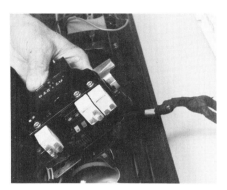

Step 3: Carefully remove timer from inside of backsplash.

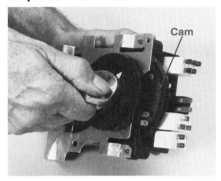

Step 4: Turn cam clockwise with knob to be sure it moves freely.

Step 5: Take knob off by first removing detent pin with needle-nose pliers or a small screwdriver. Pull knob off. Then pull off dial.

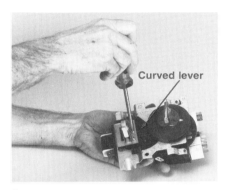

Step 6: If your model has a MINI-QUICK setting, remove its toggle and bracket by first removing two Phillips screws, then pulling curved lever off its shaft.

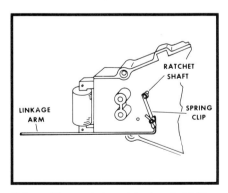

Step 7: Models with the RAPID WASH system use a spring clip and a linkage arm activated by water level switch. If your timer has this type of setting, disconnect linkage arm and pull lever off shaft.

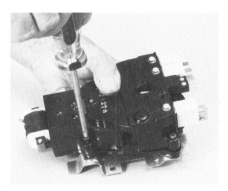

Step 8: Holding timer firmly in one hand with shaft pointed down, use a Phillips screwdriver to remove four screws which hold timer housing together.

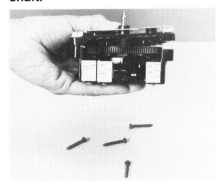

Step 9: Firmly holding timer together, turn it over (shaft up) and let four screws fall out.

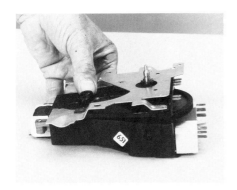

Step 10: Put timer down on a flat surface while slowly releasing your hand pressure. It will open up about ½".

Step 11: Lift timer parts off one by one, beginning with metal mounting bracket, matching each part with illustration at beginning of this procedure.

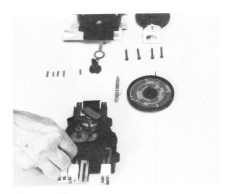

Step 12: Remove front housing, hub, compression spring, shaft, and detent spring and both printed circuit and molded cams.

Step 13: Next, remove cam followers, guide, gears, and motor.

Rotor | Field and coil

Step 14: The timer motor has two parts — the field and coil, and the rotor. If either of these parts appears damaged, it should be replaced.

Step 15: Visually check leaf switch contacts for pitting, burns, or welding. This is especially important on switches #1 and #4. Make sure that fiber spacers in #2 and #4 switches are not broken and are properly in place.

Step 16: To reassemble plastic housing timer, first place hub on rotor into yoke lamination. Fit collar at base of pinion gear into U-shaped cutout in timer housing.

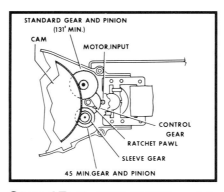

STANDARD GEAR AND PINION
(131' MIN.)
CAM
MOTOR, INPUT
CONTROL GEAR
RATCHET PAWL
SLEEVE GEAR
45 MIN. GEAR AND PINION

Step 17: On MINI-QUICK models only, use Gear and Pinion illustration to reassemble gear and shaft assemblies. Ratchet pawl should point toward timer motor. Two pinions should mesh with teeth of molded cam.

Step 18: Fit guide over center hub of timer housing with end fitting into a slot in the left side.

12 **continued**

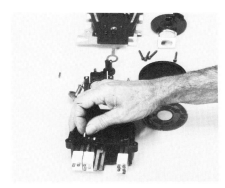

Step 19: Drop PUSH-PULL switch nylon insulator into center of hole in guide with beveled end down.

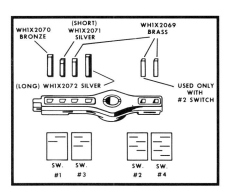

Step 20: Following above illustration, line up cam followers. This is the order they go into the holes in the guide.

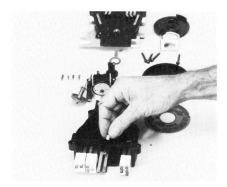

Step 21: Fit cam followers into guide holes. If there is no #2 switch on your timer, you will not have fifth follower, which is brass.

Step 22: Fit printed circuit cam into recess on back of molded cam, matching notches and lugs.

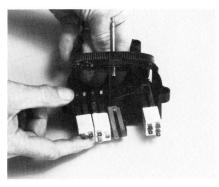

Step 23: Place cams in position over guide and followers.

Step 24: Fit timer shaft with detent spring attached down into center guide hole as shown. Then fit hub over shaft, matching flange cutouts with cam bosses.

Step 25: Turn front housing over, noting cam leaves and contacts, two balancing springs, three gear shaft holes, and a recess for compression spring. Check contacts for burns.

Step 26: Place compression spring over hub with its "fingers" pointing upward and towards end of timer.

Step 27: Place front housing over hub and press down slowly so that gear shafts will enter shaft holes.

12 continued

Step 28: Place mounting bracket on top of front housing. Gently squeeze and hold timer together until all parts are meshed together.

Step 29: Turn timer over, drop in four screws and tighten slightly. Before tightening completely, visually and by touch, check all gear shafts, motor, and compression spring for accurate location. Make sure cam turns freely. Tighten screws completely.

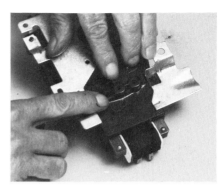

Step 30: If your timer has a MINI-QUICK switch, mount it by pressing the curved lever onto the shaft. The V cutout on bottom of toggle must straddle end of lever. Fasten toggle down with two Phillips screws.

Step 31: Slip detent pin into slots on back of knob.

Step 32: To replace dial, press it onto the hub. Pull timer shaft out and snap knob into place.

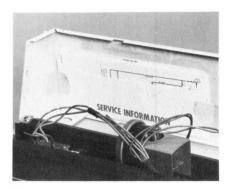

Step 33: Reconnect wires. Timer wiring label inside backsplash or appliance mini-manual can be used as reference.

Step 34: After reconnecting all wires, wind them around top of timer and then under timer motor end. Be sure that wires are not pinched. Mount timer in backsplash with three hex screws.

Step 35: Close backsplash, being careful not to pinch any wires. Return screws to backsplash. Reconnect power supply.

Notes

13 Inspecting and replacing plastic housing timer hub

Skill Level Rating:	Easy	Average	Difficult	**Very Difficult**

The washer control knob meshes with the plastic housing timer hub. The geared "teeth" of both components allow the knob to turn the hub and select a desired cycle.

Inside the timer housing, the hub fits on the timer shaft and interfaces with rotating cams that open and close the timer switches. At the bottom of the timer shaft, a small nylon insulator controls the "on-off" action of the washer. When the control knob is set for a particular cycle, and the knob is pulled out, the timer motor is activated. The timer motor drives gears, which in turn activate the rotating cams. Cam followers then activate internal switches to provide the correct washer performance sequence. When the control knob is pushed in, the nylon insulator breaks the magnetic field of the internal power switch. The switch opens and flow of current is interrupted, turning the washer off.

If the knob and hub do not mesh properly, slipping will occur, and the timer will not function properly.

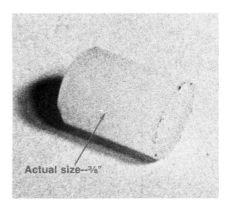

Actual size—⅜"

Nylon insulator

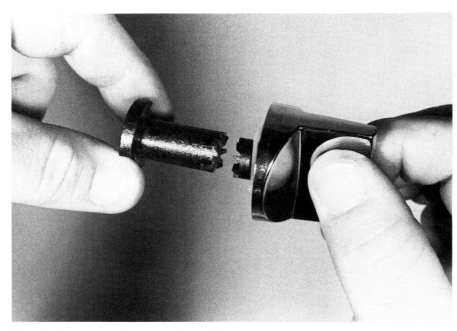

Plastic housing timer hub and knob

13 continued

Step 1: Be sure all washer controls including timer are turned **OFF**. Unplug washer from receptacle. Watch for sharp edges on parts.

Step 2: Remove three hex-head screws which hold timer to inside of backsplash.

Step 3: Disconnect wiring from timer, making note of wiring positions for reinstallation.

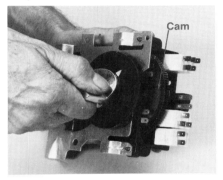

Step 4: Turn cam clockwise with knob to be sure it moves freely.

Step 5: Take knob off by first removing detent pin with needle nose pliers or a small screwdriver. Pull knob off. Then pull off dial.

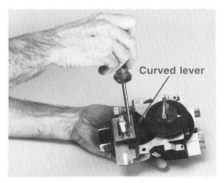

Step 6: If your model has a MINI-QUICK setting, remove its toggle and bracket by first removing two Phillips screws, then pulling curved lever off its shaft.

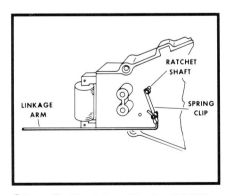

Step 7: Models with the RAPID WASH system use a spring clip and a linkage arm activated by water level switch. If your timer has this type of setting, disconnect linkage arm and pull lever off shaft.

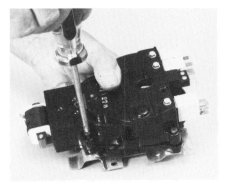

Step 8: Holding timer firmly in one hand with shaft pointed down, use a Phillips screwdriver to remove four screws which hold timer housings together.

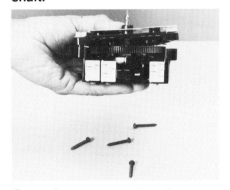

Step 9: Firmly holding timer together, turn it over (shaft up) and let four screws fall out.

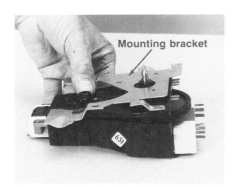

Step 10: Place timer on flat surface. Slowly release hand pressure. Timer housing will open about ½ inch.

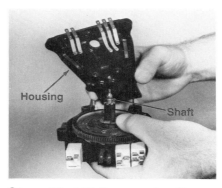

Step 11: Lift timer parts off carefully making visual comparison with illustration at beginning of procedure. Remove metal bracket and plastic front housing first.

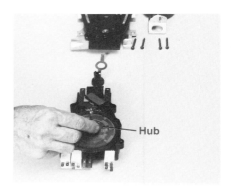

Step 12: Remove hub spring from shaft. Next, remove hub from shaft noting correct position on cams.

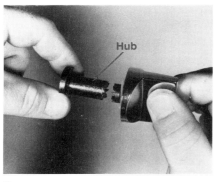

Step 13: Match hub and knob "teeth". Inspect for damage to both hub and knob that would prevent "teeth" from meshing properly.

Step 14: Should any damage to hub or knob be visible, replace with new part. Reassemble timer.

Step 15: If hub and knob "teeth" mesh properly you may want to check plastic insulator at bottom of shaft.

Step 16: Remove shaft, printed circuit cam, and molded cam. Make visual inspection of gear and cam position. Handle timer carefully so as not to disturb other components.

Step 17: Check position of nylon insulator. Beveled end should be down. Insulator must be in proper position in order to stop electrical current when knob is pushed in.

Step 18: To reassemble, fit printed circuit cam into recess on back of molded cam, matching notches and lugs. Place cams in position over guide and followers.

Step 19: Fit timer shaft with detent spring attached down into center guide hole as shown. Then fit hub over shaft, matching flange cutouts with cam bosses (stops).

Step 20: Place compression spring over hub with its "fingers" pointing upward and towards end of timer.

Step 21: Place front housing over hub and press down slowly so that gear shafts will enter shaft holes.

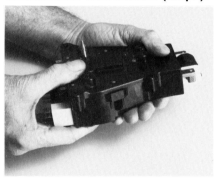

Step 22: Place mounting bracket on top of front housing. Gently squeeze and hold timer together until all parts are meshed together.

Step 23: Turn timer over, drop in four screws and tighten slightly. Before tightening completely, check gear shafts, and compression spring for accurate location. Make sure cam turns freely. Tighten screws completely.

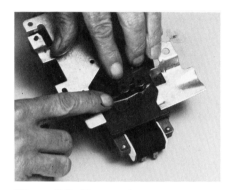

Step 24: If your timer has a MINI-QUICK switch, mount it by pressing the curved lever onto the shaft. The V cutout on bottom of toggle must straddle end of lever. Fasten toggle down with two Phillips screws.

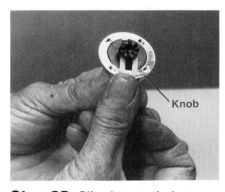

Step 25: Slip detent pin into slots on back of knob. Replace dial, pressing onto hub. Pull timer shaft out and snap knob into place.

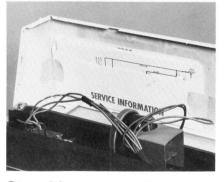

Step 26: Reconnect timer wiring. Carefully wind excess wiring aroung top of timer and under motor end so wires are not pinched.

Step 27: Remount timer in backsplash. Close backsplash carefully, being sure not to pinch any internal wiring. Replace backsplash screws and reconnect power supply.

14 Inspecting metal housing timer switches and motor

Skill Level Rating: | Easy | Average | Difficult | **Very Difficult**

There are two different types of timers used in General Electric and Hotpoint washers. Your washer will have either a metal housing timer or plastic housing timer. If your timer's outside case or "housing" is molded plastic, refer to Procedures #10-13.

The metal housing timer controls the operation of the washer's cycles. It tells the major components when to start and stop and how long to run. Each timer switch has a special function which can best be understood by referring to your washer's circuit diagram and cam chart. First, read the section of this manual titled Tools and Testing Equipment. Then, examine your washer's timer switches, circuit diagram, and cam chart. For instance, on the diagram and chart for the metal housing timer, the switches labeled 14R-15R and 19R-20R turn the drive motor on and off. The water level switch bypass which allows the motor to run during the spin sequence is controlled by the switch labeled 16R-17R. Switches labeled 5R-6R, 5R-4R, 23R-22R, and 23R-24R perform the motor reversing function to provide both spin and agitation.

All the switches and the motor in the metal housing timer can be tested without removing the timer from the backsplash. Their replacement is covered in Procedure #15: Replacing Metal Housing Timer Switches and Motor.

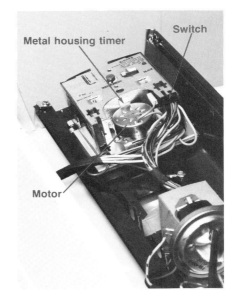

Metal housing timer (rear view)

Note: Procedures #14, #15, and #16 all deal with the metal housing timer. Timer procedures follow this sequence:
Procedure #14: Inspecting Metal Housing Timer Switches and Motor
Procedure #15: Replacing Metal Housing Timer Switches and Motor
Procedure #16: Disassembling Metal Housing Timer

SWITCH TESTING GUIDE

	OFF	BEGIN AGITATION	END AGITATION	BEGIN SPIN	BEGIN RINSE
5-4	X	C	C	O	C
5-6	X	O	O	C	O
8-7	O	O	O	O	C
8-9	O	C	C	O	O
11-10	O	O	O	O	C
11-12	X	C	C	O	O
14-15	X	C	O	C	C
17-16	X	O	O	C	O
20-19	X	O	C	O	O
23-22	X	C	C	O	C
23-24	X	O	O	C	O

O=OPEN   C=CLOSED   X=EITHER OPEN OR CLOSED

Switch testing guide

51

14 continued

Step 1: Be sure all washer controls are turned **OFF**. Unplug the washer from the receptacle. Watch for sharp edges on operating panel.

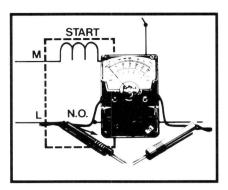

Step 2: This procedure requires the use of an ohmmeter and the ability to read a circuit diagram. For instructions, please refer to Tools and Testing Equipment, pages 101-104.

Step 3: Remove the operating panel. If you are unfamiliar with this process refer to Procedure #3: Removing Operating Panel.

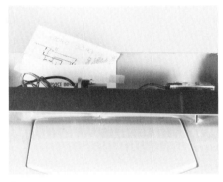

Step 4: Locate mini-manual in envelope inside washer backsplash or refer to circuit diagram in backsplash or glued to back of washer. Locate timer switches on circuit diagram and familiarize yourself with functions.

Step 5: Set ohmmeter to R x 1. Using the Switch Testing Guide shown in introduction to this procedure, test all switches with the ohmmeter. Set operating panel control knob for the different cycles as indicated on Switch Testing Guide.

Step 6: When chart indicates a switch should be open at a certain point in cycle, ohmmeter needle should show no continuity. If switch should be closed, needle should sweep upscale to indicate continuity. Example: When agitation begins, contacts 5-4 should be closed.

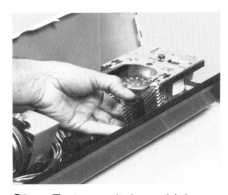

Step 7: Any switches which are faulty should be replaced by replacing entire switch bank. Refer to Procedure #15: Replacing Metal Housing Timer Switches and Motor.

Step 8: Test timer motor for continuity with ohmmeter set to R x 1. Touch one ohmmeter probe to each terminal inside block connectors. If timer motor shows no continuity, replace it.

Step 9: Reassemble washer and reconnect power supply.

15 Replacing metal housing timer switches and motor

Skill Level Rating:

Easy	Average	Difficult	**Very Difficult**

The metal housing timer has a small motor which controls the cam speed. Because of the various wash cycles and other special features, different timer motors can be found on many washer models. The timer motor as well as the switches can be replaced without removing the timer from the backsplash.

Note: Procedures #14, #15, and #16 all deal with the metal housing timer. Timer procedures follow this sequence:
Procedure #14: Inspecting Metal Housing Timer Switches and Motor
Procedure #15: Replacing Metal Housing Timer Switches and Motor
Procedure #16: Disassembling Metal Housing Timer

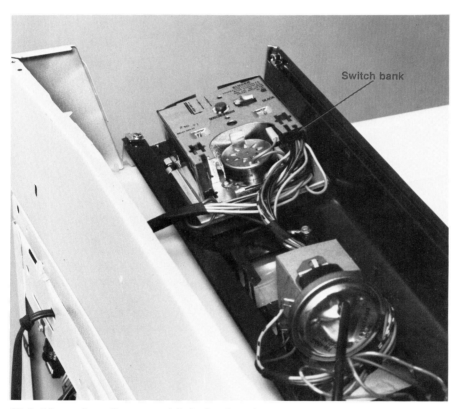

Switch bank

Metal housing timer multiple leaf switch banks and motor

15 continued

Step 1: Be sure the timer is turned **OFF**. Unplug the washer from the receptacle. Watch for sharp edges on operating panel.

Step 2: Remove the operating panel. If you are unfamiliar with this process, refer to Procedure #3: Removing Operating Panel.

Step 3: First, test all timer switches by following Procedure #14: Inspecting Metal Housing Timer Switches and Motor.

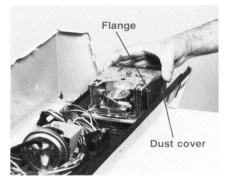

Step 4: If a switch needs to be replaced, remove dust cover around sides of timer by unhooking flange at each end with your fingers. Slide dust cover off back of timer.

Step 5: Using needle-nose pliers, straighten tab nearest switch to be removed. This allows switch to move partially out of its retaining slot.

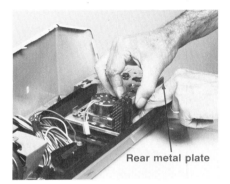

Step 6: Using your fingers, spread apart two metal plates located above and below switch. Slide switch outwards toward middle of backsplash.

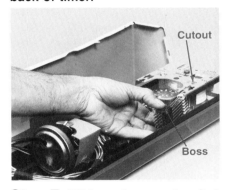

Step 7: Slide replacement switch into place, rebending tab. Make sure bosses on sides of switches are properly seated in cutouts in metal plates.

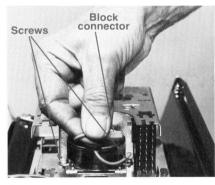

Step 8: To remove motor, remove two block connectors and two Phillips head screws.

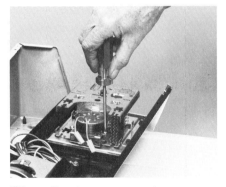

Step 9: Timer motors have model numbers. Make sure your replacement motor is exactly the same as the old one. To install new motor, replace block connectors and two screws. Reassemble washer and reconnect power supply.

16 Disassembling metal housing timer

Skill Level Rating: | Easy | Average | Difficult | **Very Difficult** |

The metal housing timer has relatively few parts, as shown in the accompanying photograph. If the problem is not in the switches or motor (determined by following Procedure #14: Inspecting Metal Housing Timer Switches and Motor), the timer must be removed from the backsplash and disassembled.

Note: Procedures #14, #15, and #16 all deal with the metal housing timer. Timer procedures follow this sequence:
Procedure #14: Inspecting Metal Housing Timer Switches and Motor
Procedure #15: Replacing Metal Housing Timer Switches and Motor
Procedure #16: Disassembling Metal Housing Timer

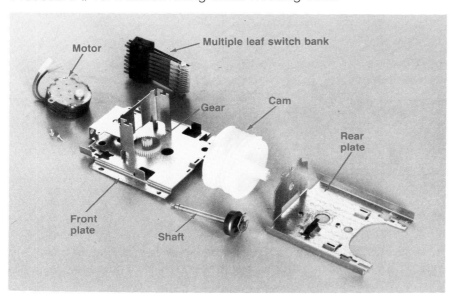

Metal housing timer (exploded view)

R 3 BLK	R 2 ORN	R 1 RED BLK
R 6 LT BLUE	R 5 WHT	R 4 YEL
R 9 TAN	R 8 BRN	R 7
R12	R11 RED-WHT	R10
R15 BRN WHT	R14 PUR	R13
R18	R17 YEL BLK	R16
R21	R20 BRN WHT	R19 PUR
R24 YEL	R23 PINK	R22 LT BLUE

Note: The above chart shows the terminal end of your timer when the shaft is pointing down. The terminals are identified by right and left-hand switches (if your model has both) and by the color of the wires attached to them.

Step 1: Be sure the timer is turned to **OFF**. Unplug the washer from the receptacle. Watch for sharp edges on access panels.

Step 2: Remove operating panel. If you are unfamiliar with this process, refer to Procedure #3: Removing Operating Panel.

Step 3: If necessary, remove dial and knob in order to free timer. Use needle-nose pliers or a small screwdriver to remove detent pin from behind knob.

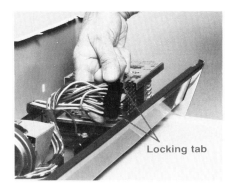

Locking tab

Step 4: Depress two locking tabs which hold terminal block in place. Pull forward on block, (not wires), to remove block from timer switch.

Screws

Step 5: To remove timer, use nutdriver to remove two hex head screws. Lift timer off rear tabs.

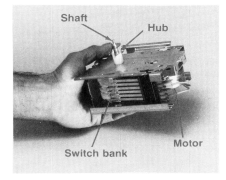

Shaft
Hub
Switch bank
Motor

Step 6: Inspect timer closely. Note shaft and hub, motor and one or two multiple leaf switch banks. Timer inside contains plastic gears and a cam. Timer back has a red hub that is part of the PUSH-PULL switch.

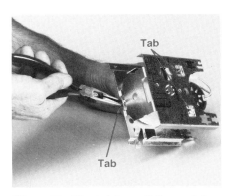

Tab
Tab

Step 7: Straighten all three tabs with needle nose pliers. Separate timer housing.

Step 8: Inspect timer for any damaged parts. Check for burned contacts, broken gears or cam. Replace any damaged part using same size and capacity as original part.

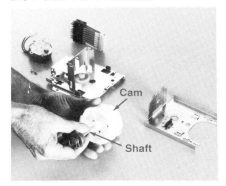

Cam
Shaft

Step 9: To reassemble timer, slide shaft through cam. Be sure detent pin is in place.

Step 10: Slip hub of cam through hole in front plate. Engage gear teeth.

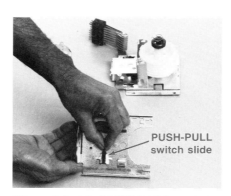

Step 11: Fit PUSH-PULL switch slide into back plate with beveled end toward middle.

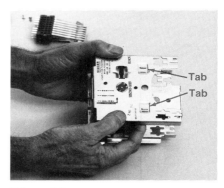

Step 12: Fit tab at opposite end from switches into its slot, while lining up rear cam hub with hole in rear plate. Now line up other two tabs with their slots and snap together. Rebend first tab.

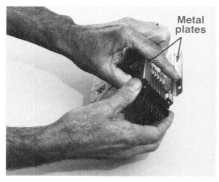

Step 13: If there is only one switch, spread plates apart slightly, and slide switch into place. Be sure both switch bosses are seated in metal plates. Rebend two remaining tabs. (With two switches, rebend tab nearest each switch).

Step 14: Turn timer so contact end of switch leaves is facing you. PUSH-PULL switch slider "finger" should be inside inverted U.

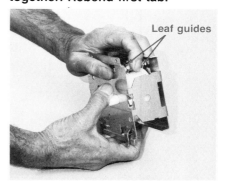

Step 15: Be sure all leaf guides are square against cam. If not, lift ends of switch leaves to clear cam rises, letting leaf guides fall freely into place. Repeat for second switch, if necessary.

Step 16: Reinstall timer motor and reconnect motor leads.

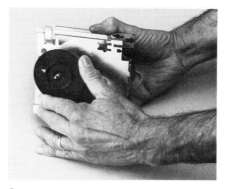

Step 17: Push the dial pointer disk onto the shaft.

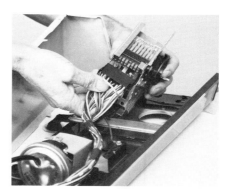

Step 18: To reinstall timer in backsplash, plug in the terminal blocks. Be sure the detents are engaged.

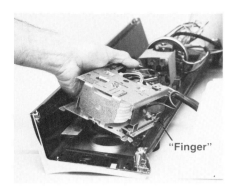

"Finger"

Step 19: Slip front plate "finger" into the slot inside the backsplash. Rotate the timer into position.

Step 20: Installing the right screw first, replace the two hex head screws at top edge of timer.

Step 21: Being sure wires are not pinched or stressed, close backsplash. Put trim parts and mounting screws into place.

Step 22: Install detent pin behind control knob. Pull timer shaft out. Fit knob over shaft and push knob onto the shaft. Reconnect power supply.

17 Inspecting and replacing cover shield

Skill Level Rating:	Easy	**Average**	Difficult	Very Difficult

The flexible plastic cover shield is attached to the underside of the cover of your washer. A rigid plastic retainer supports and correctly shapes the shield. Both the shield and retainer are held to the washer cover by a loop of wire. If the cover shield should tear, warp, fall off, or be damaged in any way, it can be easily replaced.

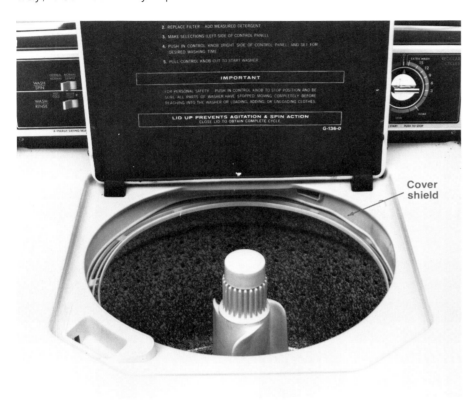

Cover shield

17 continued

Step 1: Be sure all washer controls are turned **OFF**. Unplug the washer from the receptacle. Watch for sharp edges on access panel.

Step 2: Open the top access panel. If you are not familiar with this procedure, refer to Procedure #4: Opening Washer Cover.

Step 3: Move washer away from wall to a position where cover can be raised. Lean cover back against wall in order not to overstress electrical connections and wires.

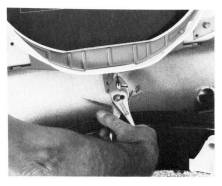

Step 4: Inspect cover shield for tears or warping. If damaged in any way, replace with new shield. To remove shield twist retaining wire counter-clockwise with pliers.

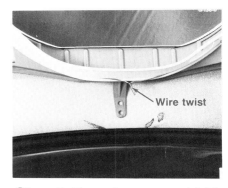

Step 5: To replace cover shield, correctly position shield and wire retainer on the cover. Wire twist should be pointing down toward the inside of washer.

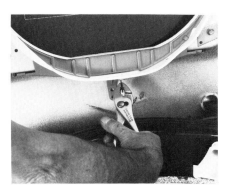

Step 6: Using pliers, twist wire retainer clockwise until tight.

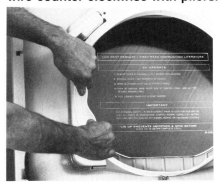

Step 7: Pull gently on the cover shield to test for tightness.

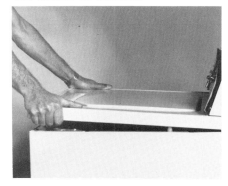

Step 8: Reassemble washer and reconnect power supply.

18 Inspecting and removing agitator

Skill Level Rating: | Easy | **Average** | Difficult | Very Difficult |

The agitator is the most visible part of the washer drive system. It is the large, finned component that connects to the transmission shaft in the center of the wash basket. The agitator's oscillating action, combined with water and detergent, washes your clothes. Design of agitators may vary slightly, but function and replacement is basically the same. Some newer models may also feature a Handwash™ agitator concealed beneath the regular agitator. The Handwash™ agitator is used for smaller, more delicate wash loads.

Note: Every 4 to 6 months, your agitator should be removed and checked for accumulated lint and adequate lubrication, as explained in your *Use & Care Book*.

A black rubber agitator mount is located between the agitator coupling and the transmission shaft. At times, the mount may come off the shaft with the agitator. A replacement transmission also comes with a mount on its shaft. When removing and replacing the agitator, be sure that there is only one rubber mount between the agitator coupling and the transmission shaft, or the agitator will not fit on the shaft properly.

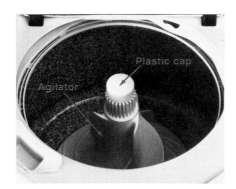
Integral filter mount agitator with plastic cap

Vinyl filter mount agitator (as seen with washer's top access cover removed)

Handwash™ agitator

Step 1: Be sure all washer controls are turned **OFF**. Unplug the washer from the receptacle.

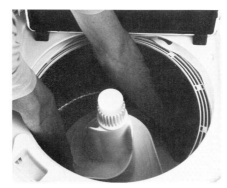
Step 2: To remove agitator, reach in with both hands under bottom of agitator. Give a sharp tug upward. If you cannot easily pull agitator out, it may be "frozen" to transmission shaft.

Step 3: To remove "frozen" vinyl filter mount agitator, use a small, thin screwdriver to loosen adhesive holding mount to agitator. Remove mount from agitator and proceed to Steps 5-6.

18 continued

Step 4: To remove "frozen" agitator on models <u>without vinyl filter mount</u>, snap off plastic cap. Cut out center web of agitator, exposing shaft and coupling. Then follow Steps 5-6.

Step 5: Pour hot water or a few drops of loosening oil on shaft and coupling.

Step 6: To remove agitator, tap lightly on agitator with hammer while pulling up. Clean and replace as in Steps 11-12.

Step 7: To access <u>Handwash™ agitator</u>, twist or rotate locking tabs as indicated to top of main agitator. Reach under bottom edge of main agitator and pull up sharply.

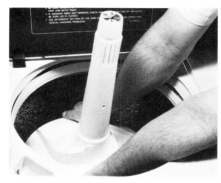

Step 8: To remove Handwash™ agitator, reach under bottom edge of agitator and pull up sharply. If agitator cannot easily be removed, it may be "frozen" to transmission shaft.

Step 9: To remove "frozen" Handwash™ agitator, first pry metal foil disc from agitator top. Note: It may be necessary to apply adhesive to disc when reinstalling agitator. Remove screw beneath disc.

Step 10: Pour a slow, steady stream of hot water or a few drops of loosening oil into screw hole. Gently tap on side of agitator with hammer while pulling up. Clean and replace as in Steps 11-12.

Step 11: Clean transmission shaft, agitator, and area beneath agitator in tub. Check transmission shaft spline for adequate lubrication. If necessary, apply bearing grease sparingly.

Step 12: To reinstall agitator, center on transmission shaft and press down firmly. Replace any screws, rings, discs, as necessary. Be sure agitator is firmly seated before reconnecting power.

19 Inspecting and replacing lid switch

Skill Level Rating:	Easy	Average	**Difficult**	Very Difficult

The lid switch on your washer is a safety device which stops the electrical power to the motor when the lid is raised. Some models have a lid switch which stops the machine completely. Other models have a lid switch which stops the power during spin only, allowing the washer to fill and agitate with the lid open.

The lid switch is located to the right of the lid. When the lid is closed, a tab on the hinge goes through a small hole in the washer cover, depressing a small pad on the switch linkage. This pad closes the lid switch and allows current to flow in a continuous circuit so that the washer cycle continues. The lid switch can be tested and replaced if it is faulty.

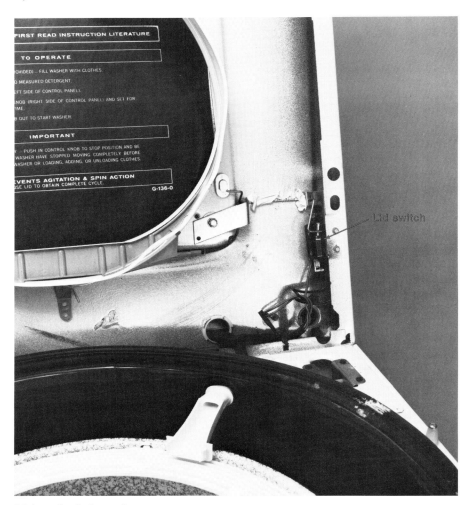

Lid switch location

19 continued

Step 1: Be sure all washer controls are turned **OFF**. Unplug the washer from the receptacle. Watch for sharp edges on access panels and parts.

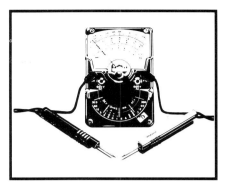

Step 2: This procedure requires the use of an ohmmeter. For instructions on how to use an ohmmeter, refer to Tools and Testing Equipment, page 101.

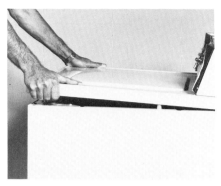

Step 3: Open washer cover. If you are unfamiliar with this procedure, refer to Procedure #4: Opening Washer Cover.

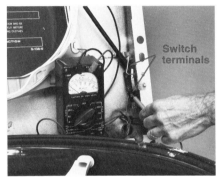

Step 4: Set ohmmeter to R x 1. Pull off one wire terminal from its switch terminal. Touch one ohmmeter probe to each switch terminal.

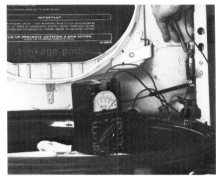

Step 5: Open lid slightly so that hinge tab is not depressing linkage pad. Activate leaf switch by pressing it down. Needle should sweep upscale to indicate continuity. If test fails, replace switch.

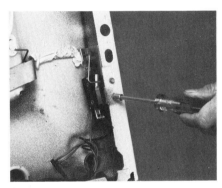

Step 6: To replace lid switch, remove 2 hex head screws with a nutdriver.

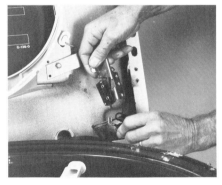

Step 7: Disconnect wire terminals. For installation reference, make note of how wires are connected.

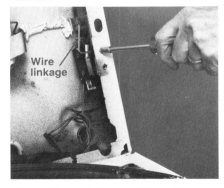

Step 8: Install new lid switch with the 2 hex head screws. Reconnect wire terminals. Be sure that the new switch bracket properly supports the wire linkage.

Step 9: Reassemble washer and reconnect power supply.

20 Inspecting and replacing transmission boot

Skill Level Rating: | Easy | Average | Difficult | **Very Difficult** |

The transmission boot is a large, circular, rubber component. The boot is clamped tightly to the base of the tub and the top of the transmission. It serves as a flexible water seal between the stationary and moving systems of the washer. It also prevents water from leaking out of the bottom of your washer.

Transmission boot (basket removed)

Step 1 : Be sure all washer controls are turned **OFF**. Unplug the washer from the receptacle. Watch for sharp edges.

Step 2: Visually inspect floor around washer for leaks. If washer leaks, check all inlet and discharge hoses and connections. If these are not faulty, the boot may be damaged and should be replaced.

Step 3: To replace boot, open washer cover. If you are unfamiliar with this process, refer to Procedure #4: Opening Washer Cover.

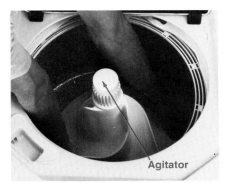

Agitator

Step 4: Remove agitator from middle of washer basket. If you are unfamiliar with this process, refer to Procedure #18: Inspecting and Replacing Agitator.

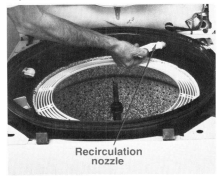

Recirculation nozzle

Step 5: Remove recirculation nozzle by pulling it off.

Basket boot (hub boot)

Step 6: Remove plastic basket boot (or hub boot) by releasing spring-loaded tab. Lift basket boot straight up and off transmission shaft.

Step 7: Removing basket boot exposes 3 bolts that hold washer basket in machine. Remove these 3 bolts using a 12 point, 1/2 inch socket with short extension and ratchet.

Basket

Step 8: Lift washer basket up and out of washer. Be careful not to dislodge the nozzles around top of washer.

Step 9: Large rubber transmission boot is now visible. Inspect boot for damage. Watch for sharp, pointed objects.

20 continued

Step 10: To replace transmission boot, loosen two clamps, upper and lower, which hold boot in place. Use nutdriver or small socket with extension.

Step 11: Grasp under rubber boot and pull up sharply with both hands. Lift boot out of washer.

Step 12: Remove circular metal clamp rings from old transmission boot. Wipe rings clean and fit onto new boot.

Step 13: Wipe tub bottom dry. Push boot into place with lower clamp screw positioned near drain hole. Tighten all clamps. If clamps are difficult to tighten, use a soap solution to lubricate clamp screw. Be sure boot is properly seated.

Step 14: Carefully lower washer basket back into tub. Be careful not to dislodge nozzles near top of washer.

Step 15: Replace three basket bolts using a 12 point, 1/2 inch socket with a short extension and a ratchet.

Step 16: Replace basket boot by lowering boot down transmission shaft and snapping boot into place. Make sure spring-loaded tab is engaged. Grease shaft spline lightly.

Step17: Replace agitator by pushing it firmly down onto transmission shaft. Make sure agitator is properly seated.

Step 18: Replace washer cover. Be sure to pull recirculation nozzle back through its opening in cover shield. Reconnect power supply.

Notes

21 Inspecting and replacing transmission

Skill Level Rating: | Easy | Average | Difficult | **Very Difficult** |

The transmission sends power from the motor to the agitator and wash basket. This power provides both agitation and spin, depending on which direction the input pulley is being driven by the belt attached to the underside of the transmission.

If your washer appears to be leaking oil, or if the agitation or spin functions are not occurring, you may need to replace your transmission.

Note: This procedure requires referral to Procedure #20: Inspecting and Replacing Transmission Boot to disassemble the washer for access to the transmission and reassembly of the washer after transmission replacement.

Transmission (boot removed)

Step 1: Be sure all washer controls are turned **OFF**. Unplug the washer from the receptacle. Watch for sharp edges.

Step 2: Transmission boot must be removed before replacing transmission. Refer to Procedure #20: Inspecting and Replacing Transmission Boot, Steps 1 through 11.

Step 3: With transmission boot removed from washer, locate six ³⁄₈-inch hex bolts which anchor transmission. There are three bolts on either side of transmission.

Step 4: Remove all six bolts from transmission. Save for reuse. Use a ⅜″ socket with a long extension.

Step 5: Slide transmission to rear of washer to free belt. Inspect belt for damage. Lift transmission up. Caution: Transmission is heavy.

Step 6: Drop first bolt in right rear hole in replacement transmission and lower transmission into washer.

Step 7: Turning by hand, screw first bolt into suspension, but do not tighten. Using this bolt as a pivot, swing transmission to right rear of washer.

Step 8: With one hand, install belt in its groove around transmission pulley.

Step 9: To properly align remaining five bolts, insert Phillips screwdriver in left front hole of transmission flange and suspension speed nut. Swing transmission to left front of washer.

Step 10: Using a ⅜″ socket, install four bolts in four open holes.

Step 11: Remove screwdriver and install last bolt. Tighten all six bolts securely.

Step 12: To completely reassemble from this point, refer to Steps 12-18 in Procedure #20: Inspecting and Replacing Transmission Boot.

22 Inspecting and replacing motor start relay

Skill Level Rating: | Easy | Average | Difficult | **Very Difficult** |

The motor start relay is an external switch which sends current to the start windings in the main motor just long enough to get it started. The accompanying partial circuit diagram shows the relationship between the motor and relay. (For additional help in understanding a circuit diagram, refer to Tools and Testing Equipment at the end of this manual.) When current first enters the washer, only the relay coil and the run winding of the motor are energized. The relay switch contacts are open so that there is no current in the start winding. The run winding of the motor and the relay coil draw high current, creating a strong magnetic field. The magnetic field causes the relay contacts to close, energizing the start winding.

The start winding then gives the motor power, and the motor starts to turn. As the motor speed increases, the current in the run winding and relay coil drops, and the magnetic field collapses, opening the relay contacts and stopping current to the start winding. The motor start relay could be faulty if, during normal operation, your washer runs for a few seconds and then stops, or the main motor hums but won't run.

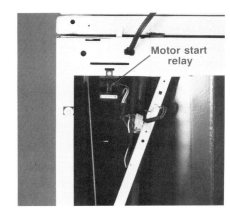

Motor start relay

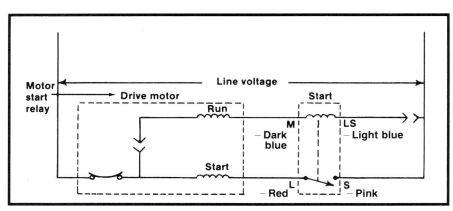

Motor start relay circuit diagram

Step 1: Be sure all washer controls are turned **OFF**. Unplug the washer from the receptacle. Watch for sharp edges on access panels and parts.

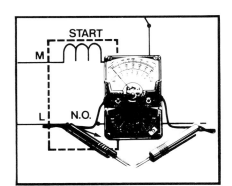

Step 2: This procedure requires the use of an ohmmeter and the ability to read a circuit diagram. For instructions, refer to Tools and Testing Equipment, pages 101-104.

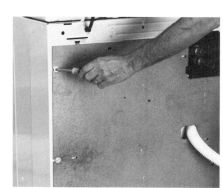

Step 3: Remove the rear access panel. If you are not familiar with this procedure, refer to Procedure #5: Removing Rear Access Panel.

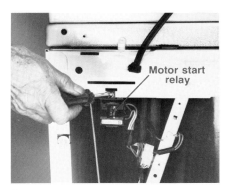

Step 4: Locate motor start relay and remove mounting screw.

Step 5: Remove wiring connections from relay, making note of position for reinstallation reference.

Step 6: Set ohmmeter on R x 1. Test coil terminals marked M-LS for continuity by placing one probe on terminal marked M and other probe on terminal marked LS. Needle should move, indicating continuity.

Step 7: Set ohmmeter on R x 1. Test coil terminals marked L-S with relay in upright position. (Arrow on relay should point up). Place one ohmmeter probe on L terminal and one probe on S terminal. Needle should not move, indicating no continuity.

Step 8: Turn relay upside down and listen to determine whether contacts click closed.

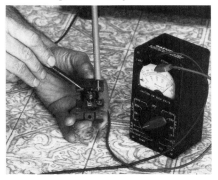

Step 9: To verify continuity, set ohmmeter for R x 1. Test L-S contacts with relay upside down by placing one probe on L terminal and one probe on S terminal. Needle should sweep upscale, indicating continuity.

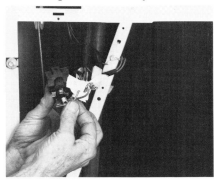

Step 10: If relay is not defective reinstall original wires.

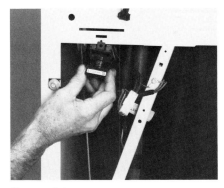

Step 11: If motor start relay is defective, be sure replacement is exactly the same as original. Reinstall wires. Clip new relay back into hole and replace mounting screw.

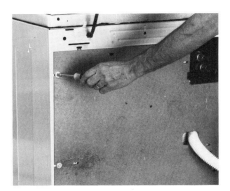

Step 12: Reassemble washer and reconnect power supply.

23 Inspecting and replacing water inlet valve

Skill Level Rating:	Easy	Average	**Difficult**	Very Difficult

The water inlet valve, or mixing valve, is a solenoid-operated component that allows hot and cold water to enter the washer through an internal chamber where both water temperatures are mixed for a warm wash. The selector switch and timer tell the valve which solenoid to actuate--hot, cold, or both. The water inlet valve is on the back of your washer, with hot and cold designated by "H" and "C." Each side of the valve has a small screen, either metal or plastic, which is replaceable. The valve itself must be replaced as a complete assembly.

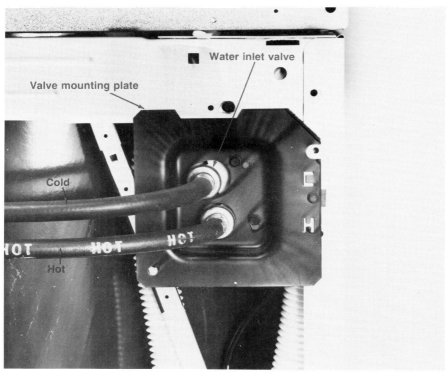

Water inlet valve

Step 1: Be sure all washer controls are turned **OFF**. Turn off faucets. Unplug the washer from the receptacle. Watch for sharp edges.

Step 2: This procedure requires the use of an ohmmeter. For instructions on how to use an ohmmeter, refer to Tools and Testing Equipment, page 101.

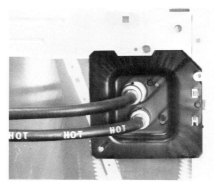

Step 3: Water inlet valve is located on back of washer. It is not necessary to remove rear access panel to test or repair valve.

Step 4: Turn faucets off. Remove intake hoses which bring water into washer from hot and cold inlets. Check hoses for kinks or deterioration.

Step 5: If water is entering your washer too slowly, inspect valve screens for damage or clogging. Determine whether your valve's screens are plastic or metal. Plastic screens can be replaced with metal, however metal cannot be replaced with plastic.

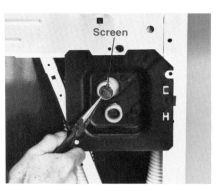

Step 6: To clean or replace water inlet valve screens, remove carefully with needle-nose pliers.

Step 7: If your hoses have screens at the ends where they attach to the faucets, check the screens for damage or clogging to assure optimum water flow.

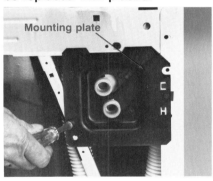

Step 8: To test or remove water inlet valve, first unscrew valve mounting plate with nutdriver.

Step 9: To test solenoids, set ohmmeter at R x 100. Remove one wire from each wire terminal and put probes across solenoid terminals. Needle will sweep upscale indicating continuity. Test both hot and cold water solenoid switch.

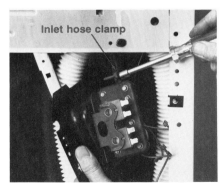

Step 10: If either solenoid test fails, replace water inlet valve. To replace valve, loosen inlet hose clamp above valve.

Step 11: Remove water inlet valve mounting screws. Remove valve from mounting plate.

Step 12: Correctly position replacement valve and install wires, screws and mounting plate. Reassemble washer and reconnect power supply.

24 Inspecting and replacing belt

Skill Level Rating: | Easy | Average | **Difficult** | Very Difficult |

The drive belt connects the clutch and the transmission. The belt also drives the transmission, which powers the agitator and the spinning basket. The tension on the drive belt can be adjusted, or the belt can be replaced.

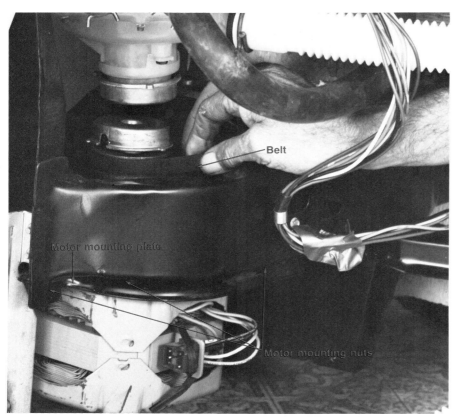

Belt

Step 1: Be sure all washer controls are turned **OFF**. Unplug the washer from the receptacle. Watch for sharp edges on access panels and parts.

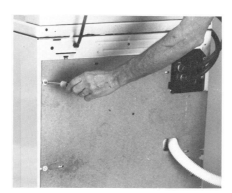

Step 2: Remove rear access panel. If you are not familiar with this process, refer to Procedure #5: Removing Rear Access Panel.

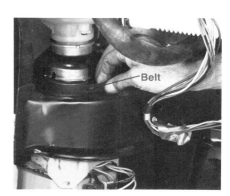

Step 3: Visually inspect belt for damage or looseness. It is correctly tightened when it can be deflected approximately ½ inch with the fingers. If it can be pushed in more than this at mid-point between pulleys, it is too loose and must be adjusted.

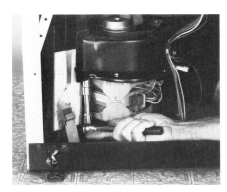

Step 4: To tighten belt, loosen but do not remove three nuts on motor mounting plate using socket and ratchet.

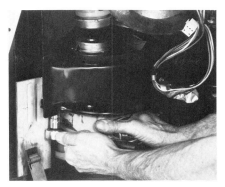

Step 5: Pull motor to rear with one hand. Do not use any type of lever. Lock in position by tightening left nut first.

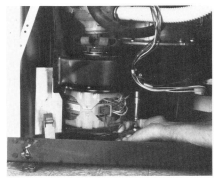

Step 6: Tighten remaining two nuts. This will increase tension on belt. Test belt for ½-inch deflection as in Step 3.

Step 7: To replace worn or damaged belt, remove upper clamp from pump coupling.

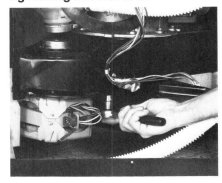

Step 8: Using socket and ratchet, loosen but do not remove three nuts on motor mounting plate.

Step 9: Remove old belt and fit new belt into transmission and clutch drum pulley grooves.

Step 10: Using one hand, pull motor to rear of washer. Do not use any type of lever. Tighten left nut first.

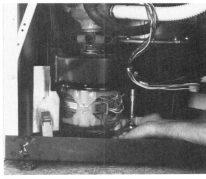

Step 11: Now tighten two front nuts. Recheck belt for proper tension. (See Step 3).

Step 12: Reassemble pump coupling and clamp. Reassemble washer and reconnect power supply.

25 Inspecting and replacing pump coupling

Skill Level Rating: | Easy | Average | **Difficult** | Very Difficult |

The pump coupling is made of a flexible rubber/fabric material. It connects the drive plate on the bottom of the pump to the drive plate on top of the clutch. If the pump coupling is worn or damaged, it can be replaced.

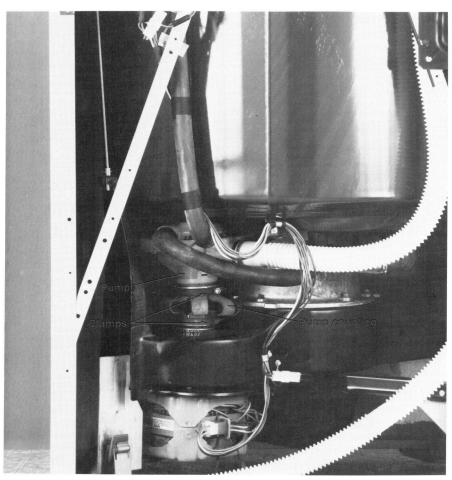

Pump coupling

Step 1: Be sure all washer controls are turned **OFF**. Unplug the washer from the receptacle. Watch for sharp edges on access panels and parts.

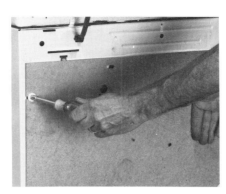

Step 2: Remove the rear access panel. If you are unfamiliar with this process, refer to Procedure #5: Removing Rear Access Panel.

Step 3: Visually inspect pump coupling for wear damage or tears in fabric. To replace, use a nutdriver to remove upper and lower clamps holding pump coupling to pump and motor.

Step 4: Remove old coupling from drive plates.

Step 5: Before installing new pump coupling, rotate pump drive plate by hand to insure that pump is not binding or is not jammed. Put both clamps over end of new coupling.

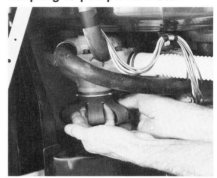

Step 6: Do not remove staples on new coupling. Using both hands, carefully fit coupling over pump drive plate, making sure it's tight and evenly seated all around.

Step 7: Put clamp screw over edge of coupling where it is stapled together. With nutdriver, tighten upper clamp around coupling and pump drive plate.

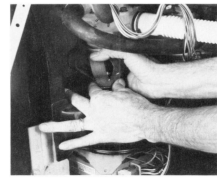

Step 8: Using both hands, fit bottom of coupling around clutch drive plate, making sure it's tight and evenly seated.

Step 9: Put clamp screw over edge of coupling where it is stapled together. With nutdriver, tighten lower clamp around bottom of coupling. Reassemble washer and reconnect power supply.

26 Inspecting and replacing pump

Skill Level Rating: | Easy | Average | **Difficult** | Very Difficult |

The pump is the main component in your washer's recirculation system. It pumps water out of the washer during the spin cycle and recirculates it during the wash and rinse cycles. The pump is driven by the motor through the pump coupling which joins the motor and pump.

There are two separate chambers in the pump, top and bottom. Each chamber has its own impeller. The upper cavity takes water from the tub and recirculates it through the machine during wash and rinse. With the motor and pump turning clockwise, the water is pulled in through one port and pushed out the other by the small impeller inside. The water then flows up through the recirculation hose and out the recirculation nozzle and through the lint filter. Water enters the lower pump chamber during the drain and spin cycle. It enters one port of the chamber and is forced out the other by the large impeller and out through the drain hose.

Note: A few models may have a non-recirculating pump with only two hoses connected to it. Service is the same for all pumps.

Pump

26 continued

Step 1: Be sure all washer controls are turned **OFF**. Unplug the washer from the receptacle. Watch for sharp edges on access panels and parts.

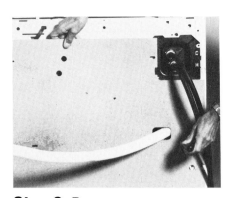

Step 2: Remove rear access panel. If you are unfamiliar with this process, refer to Procedure #5: Removing Rear Access Panel. Locate pump.

Step 3: If washer runs, but water does not drain, inspect drain hose for kinks or clogging. If problem is not with hose, check pump coupling.

Step 4: Visually inspect pump coupling for damage. If coupling needs replacement, refer to Procedure #25: Inspecting and Replacing Pump Coupling. If coupling is not the problem, pump may be jammed with a foreign object or may have a defective seal or impeller.

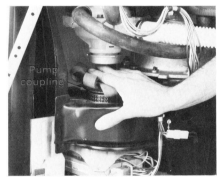

Step 5: To remove pump, use a nutdriver or ratchet to remove upper clamp from pump coupling. Push coupling down and out of the way.

Step 6: Using ratchet, remove three mounting screws that suspend pump from bottom of outer tub. Note: Do not loosen screws holding upper and lower chambers together. Lift pump out.

Step 7: Before removing hoses, be prepared to catch water trapped in washer. Remove hoses connected to pump with hose clamp pliers. Check pump for foreign objects or defects.

Step 8: Install new pump by replacing tub hoses first and then three mounting screws. Replace pump coupling and upper clamp.

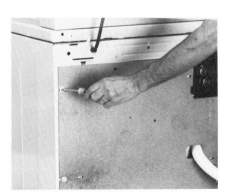

Step 9: Reassemble washer and reconnect power supply.

27 Inspecting and replacing single speed clutch

Skill Level Rating:	Easy	Average	Difficult	**Very Difficult**

The clutch is an important part of your washer's drive system. Some models have a single speed clutch, and some have a two-speed clutch which allows for a slow speed (See Procedure #28). The clutch transfers power from the motor to the transmission through the drive belt.

The clutch parts are built up separately on the motor shaft so there is no pre-assembled clutch assembly. The clutch operates centrifugally as the two primary shoes inside the drum are forced out against the drum wall, causing the drum to move at motor speed and drive the belt.

If the washer basket is not spinning fast enough, or if there is excessive noise when the washer is operating, the clutch may be faulty, and parts of it may need to be replaced.

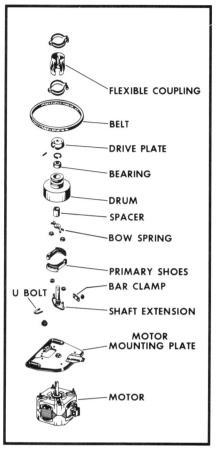

Single speed clutch
(exploded view)

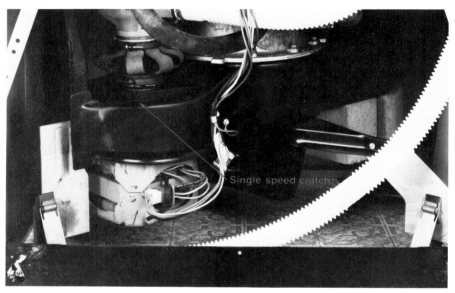

Single speed clutch

Step 1: Be sure all washer controls are turned **OFF**. Unplug the washer from the receptacle. Watch for sharp edges on access panels and parts.

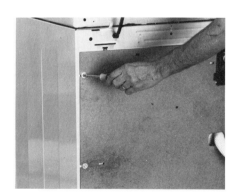

Step 2: Remove rear access panel and locate clutch. If you are unfamiliar with removing the rear access panel, refer to Procedure #5: Removing Rear Access Panel.

Step 3: Determine whether you have a single or a two-speed clutch. For two-speed clutch, see Procedure #28: Inspecting and Replacing Two-Speed Clutch.

81

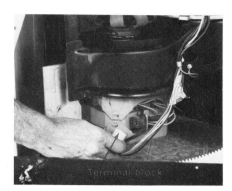

Step 4: To remove motor and clutch from washer, unplug terminal block at motor. You must remove motor to inspect and replace clutch.

Step 5: Remove lower clamp on pump coupling.

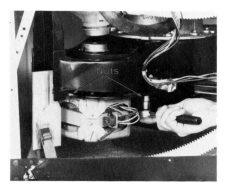

Step 6: Using a socket and ratchet, remove three nuts securing motor mounting plate to suspension.

Step 7: Remove belt from clutch pulley. Lower motor and clutch to floor.

Step 8: Tilt machine forward. Slide motor and clutch out from under washer. As you disassemble clutch, check each part for wear or damage.

Step 9: Replace any defective parts. Using a drive pin tool (which can be purchased from your authorized local appliance parts dealer) and a hammer, remove roll pin holding clutch drive plate to shaft extension. Lift drive plate off.

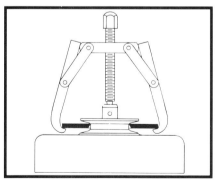

Step 10: Remove clutch drum. If drum is difficult to remove, use a horseshoe collar tool and puller (both of which can be purchased from your authorized local appliance parts dealer) to pull it off.

Step 11: If clutch drum or its bearing is damaged and needs to be replaced, remove retaining ring first by slipping it out with small screwdriver.

Step 12: Drive bearing out top of drum using small block of wood and hammer.

27 continued

Step 13: Lift off spacer and bow spring which fits over two pins that hold primary shoes.

Step 14: Remove small washers on both pins.

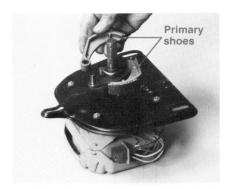

Step 15: Lift off both primary shoes and check for wear or damage. Note: Replace both shoes if either shoe is worn or damaged. Note marking showing which side should face up.

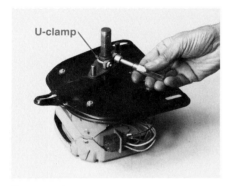

Step 16: Inspect motor shaft extension for damage such as wear or corrosion. If shaft needs to be replaced, loosen screws on U-clamp with hex head nutdriver and lift off entire motor shaft extension assembly. If shaft extension is stuck to motor shaft, tap it sharply sideways to help break it loose.

Step 17: To reassemble clutch, fit extension assembly over motor shaft, replacing old U-clamp if defective.

Step 18: Inspect bar clamp. If it is worn on one side, reverse it and reinstall it, making sure it is against flat side of motor shaft.

Step 19: Install primary shoes on pins, making sure side marked "Top" is up. Also, be sure shoes can swing freely on their pins out and away from clutch.

Step 20: Place one washer on top of each pin.

Step 21: Place bow spring and spacer over shaft and on top of washers.

Step 22: Fit clutch drum over shaft, making sure it is seated properly.

Step 23: Press down on clutch drive plate and line up holes in plate hub and shaft extension. Insert small nail or stiff wire to keep holes in line. From other side of drive plate, tap roll pin into place and at same time force out nail or wire. Drive pin all the way into place.

Step 24: To reinstall motor and clutch in washer, tilt washer forward. Slide motor and clutch into place.

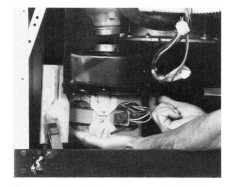

Step 25: Lift motor and clutch up onto the three studs in suspension. Screw on the three nuts by hand.

Step 26: Fit belt around transmission and clutch drum pulley grooves.

Step 27: Pull on motor with one hand and tighten left mounting nut first. Do not use any type of lever.

Step 28: Tighten other two nuts and check to be sure belt is correctly tightened. Be sure it cannot be deflected more than about 1/2 inch with the fingers.

Step 29: Reassemble pump coupling and its clamp. Reassemble washer and reconnect power supply.

28 Inspecting and replacing two-speed clutch

Skill Level Rating:	Easy	Average	Difficult	**Very Difficult**

General Electric and Hotpoint washers with both a normal speed and a slow, or gentle speed have a two-speed clutch. Like the one speed clutch, it transfers power from the motor to the transmission through the drive belt.

When energized, the two-speed clutch shifter, described in Procedure #29, slows the washer's speed as power is transferred to the agitator and washer basket. Four different sets of shoes work together to control this speed. The outer drum contains a pair of slip shoes, the inner drum contains a pair of primary shoes, and the carrier plate has two sets of lock-in shoes mounted to it. When the motor is running at full speed, the primary shoes and inner drum are also at full speed. The shoes on the carrier plate lock the inner drum to the outer drum through centrifugal force. One set of shoes moves in and one moves out. If the shifter is energized before the motor is started, the primary shoes and the inner drum still operate at the motor speed, but the carrier plate assembly is prevented from rotating when its tab and the shifter catch arm make contact. There is no centrifugal force to engage the inner and the outer lock-in shoes. The slip shoes in the outer drum will start to move away from the inner drum, maintaining just enough contact to control the speed at a slow rate.

Two-speed clutch

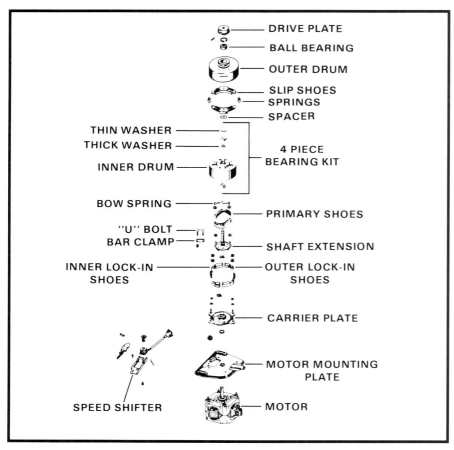

Two-speed clutch (exploded view)

Step 1: Be sure all washer controls are turned **OFF**. Unplug the washer from the receptacle. Watch for sharp edges on access panels and parts.

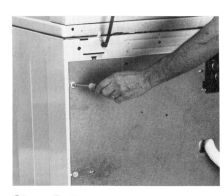

Step 2: Remove the rear access panel and locate clutch. If you are unfamiliar with removing the rear access panel, refer to Procedure #5: Removing Rear Access Panel.

Step 3: Determine whether you have a single or a two-speed clutch. For single speed clutch, see Procedure #27: Inspecting and Replacing Single Speed Clutch.

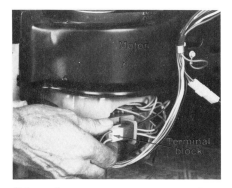

Step 4: To remove motor and clutch assembly from your washer, disconnect terminal block at motor. Note: You must remove motor to inspect and replace clutch.

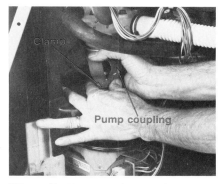

Step 5: Remove lower clamp on pump coupling.

Step 6: Using a ratchet, remove three nuts securing motor mounting plate to suspension.

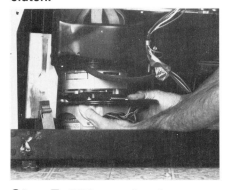

Step 7: With your hands, remove belt from clutch pulley. Tilt washer to front. Lower motor and clutch assembly out bottom of washer.

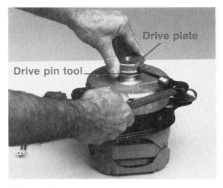

Step 8: As you disassemble clutch, check each part for wear or damage, replacing any defective parts. Using a drive pin tool and a ball peen hammer, remove roll pin holding clutch drive plate to shaft extension. Lift drive plate off.

Step 9: Locate two slip shoe lugs protruding through openings on side of outer drum wall. Insert small pin or nail down into each lug to hold slip shoes against outside of drum wall.

28 continued

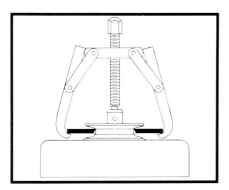

Step 10: Remove clutch drum. If drum is difficult to remove, use a horseshoe collar tool and puller, (both of which can be purchased from your local appliance parts dealer) to pull it off.

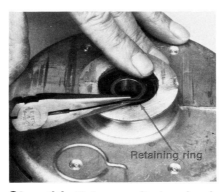

Step 11: If drum or its bearing is damaged and needs to be replaced, remove retaining ring first with needle-nose pliers.

Step 12: Drive bearing out top of drum using small block of wood and hammer.

Step 13: Inspect slip shoes held inside drum wall for wear. Note: Replace as a pair if one or both are damaged.

Step 14: Remove top half of bearing from center of inner drum and lift off the drum.

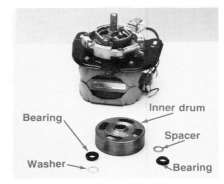

Step 15: Lift off bottom half of bearing and inspect both halves for wear or damage. There is also a spacer between two halves of bearing. To replace faulty bearings, purchase a bearing kit for two-speed clutch inner drum.

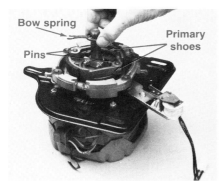

Step 16: Remove bow spring which fits over two pins holding primary shoes.

Step 17: Remove small washer on each pin.

Step 18: Lift off both primary shoes and check for wear or damage. Note: Replace both shoes if either shoe is worn or damaged. Note marking showing which side should face up.

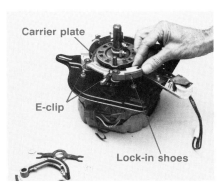

Step 19: Inspect carrier plate and its lock-in shoes for wear. Replace shoes by the pair if necessary, removing E-clip which holds shoes to plate.

Step 20: Rotate carrier plate to be sure it turns freely by turning the lock-in shoes as shown. If it does not, bearing is defective.

Step 21: Remove whole carrier plate and shaft extension assembly by removing U-bolt, two nuts, and bar clamp. Lift off carrier plate.

Step 22: Invert carrier plate and extension shaft assembly. Remove retainer clip which secures carrier plate to extension shaft.

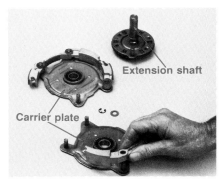

Step 23: Transfer shoes from old carrier plate to new plate.

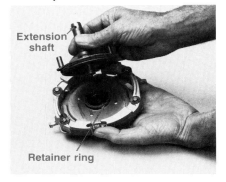

Step 24: To reassemble clutch, reinstall extension shaft and retainer ring into carrier plate.

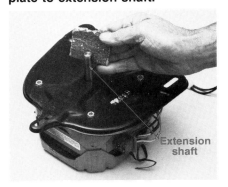

Step 25: Before putting extension shaft back onto motor shaft, lightly sandpaper motor shaft so extension shaft gives better fit.

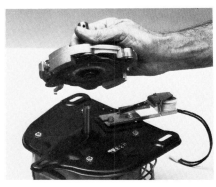

Step 26: Fit extension all the way down over motor shaft, matching open window and flat side of motor shaft. Reassemble U-bolt, bar clamp, and nuts.

Step 27: Put washers on extension shaft pins and install primary shoes, making sure side marked "TOP" is up. Also be sure that shoes can swing freely on pins, out and away from clutch.

28 continued

Step 28: Drop two washers on top of clutch shoes and put bow spring on top.

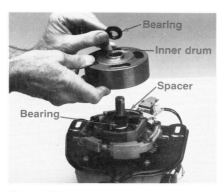

Step 29: Put bottom half of bearing on extension shaft, then spacer, then inner drum with upper half of bearing on top of it, then washer.

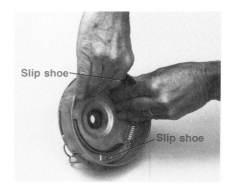

Step 30: To reinstall slip shoes in outer drum, reinsert pins described in Step 9 (if they've been removed) by pulling shoes back hard against outer drum walls so that lugs protrude.

Step 31: Press drum down over shaft, making sure it's completely seated.

Step 32: Press down on drive plate and line up holes in plate hub and shaft extension. Insert small nail or stiff wire to keep holes in line. From other side of drive plate tap roll pin into place, at the same time forcing out nail or wire. Drive pin all the way in.

Step 33: Be sure speed shifter is properly adjusted before reinstalling motor and clutch in washer. Refer to Procedure #29: Inspecting and Replacing Two-Speed Clutch Shifter.

Step 34: Remove any pins or nails that held slip shoes against drum.

Step 35: To reinstall motor and clutch in washer, tilt washer forward and slide motor and clutch into place.

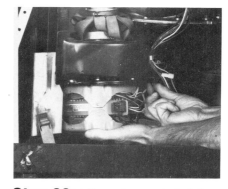

Step 36: Lift motor and clutch up on to three studs in suspension and screw on three nuts by hand.

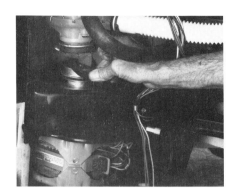

Step 37: Fit belt around transmission and clutch drum pulley grooves.

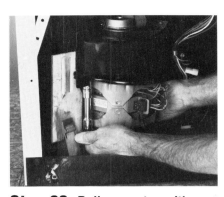

Step 38: Pull on motor with one hand and tighten left mounting nut first. Do not use any type of lever.

Step 39: Tighten other two nuts and check to be sure belt is correctly tightened. Be sure it cannot be deflected more than ½ inch with fingers.

Step 40: Reassemble pump coupling and its clamp and replace rear access panel. Reconnect power supply.

29 Inspecting and replacing two-speed clutch shifter

Skill Level Rating: | Easy | Average | Difficult | **Very Difficult** |

The shifter for the two-speed clutch is a solenoid-operated device. When the solenoid is energized, it provides gentle agitation and/or slow spin by raising a catch arm lever which prevents the lower carrier plate assembly from beginning to turn. The shifter is controlled by the selector switch on the operating panel or by the position of the timer dial.

If the slow speed on your washer is not operating properly, the problem could be a defective solenoid coil or an improperly adjusted shifter assembly. The shifter can be either adjusted or replaced.

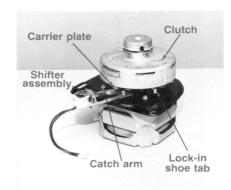

Two-speed clutch shifter

Step 1: Be sure all washer controls are turned **OFF**. Unplug washer from receptacle. Watch for sharp edges on access panels and parts.

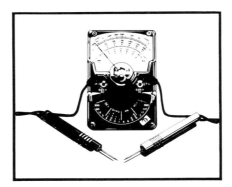

Step 2: This procedure requires the use of an ohmmeter. For instructions on how to use an ohmmeter, refer to Tools and Testing Equipment, page 101.

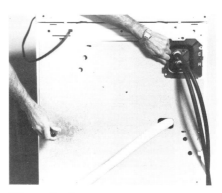

Step 3: Remove rear access panel. If you are unfamiliar with this process, refer to Procedure #5: Removing Rear Access Panel.

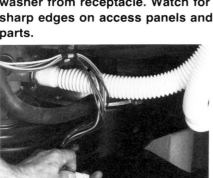

Step 4: To test shifter, disconnect two parts of plastic disconnect block on wires running up to speed selector switch.

Step 5: Set ohmmeter to R x 100. Check for resistance through shifter coil at disconnect block with ohmmeter probes. The needle should show some movement.

Step 6: If the coil is defective, refer to Procedure #28: Inspecting and Replacing Two-Speed Clutch, Steps 4-7, to remove motor and clutch. To replace coil, remove screw from under coil and slip coil out. Replace with new coil.

Step 7: If test shows coil is not defective, check catch arm. Depress catch arm above solenoid to see if other end makes contact with one of two tabs protruding from bottom of clutch.

Step 8: If tab and catch arm make contact, the problem could be that no power is being applied by selector switches. See Procedure #8: Inspecting and Replacing Selector Switches.

Step 9: If tab is not making contact when end of catch arm is raised, adjust shifter assembly by loosening two hex-head screws and moving mounting bracket in or out slightly.

Step 10: If slight bend in catch arm prevents it from making contact, adjust arm with needle-nose pliers. Do not overbend catch arm so that solenoid will not pull in properly.

Spring

Step 11: If catch arm is badly bent or damaged, replace it. Remove two springs to release catch arm.

Step 12: If necessary on your model, straighten two tabs on top of catch arm assembly so arm can be lifted off.

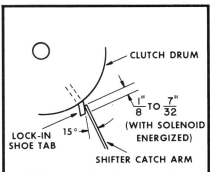

CLUTCH DRUM

$\frac{1"}{8}$ TO $\frac{7"}{32}$ (WITH SOLENOID ENERGIZED)

LOCK-IN SHOE TAB 15°

SHIFTER CATCH ARM

Step 13: When reinstalling, be sure there is ⅛-inch overlap between end of catch arm and tab.

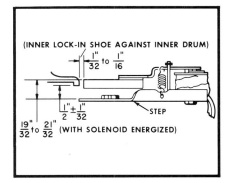

(INNER LOCK-IN SHOE AGAINST INNER DRUM)

$\frac{1"}{32}$ to $\frac{1"}{16}$

$\frac{1"}{2} \pm \frac{1"}{32}$

STEP

$\frac{19"}{32}$ to $\frac{21"}{32}$ (WITH SOLENOID ENERGIZED)

Step 14: Be sure shifter is properly adjusted according to illustrated dimensions before reinstalling and tightening screws completely.

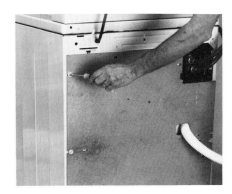

Step 15: Reassemble washer and reconnect power supply.

30 Inspecting and replacing drive motor

Skill Level Rating: | Easy | Average | Difficult | **Very Difficult** |

The motor is the most important component in the washer drive system. Current enters the washer through the line cord and powers the motor. It then in turn drives the clutch, belt, transmission and agitator.

The action of the drive motor is reversible through switches in the timer to provide for both agitation and spin. The motor has both a start winding and a run winding. The run winding, the larger wire, is in the circuit continuously. The start winding, the smaller wire, energizes only briefly, just long enough to start the motor turning. An external motor start relay, described in Procedure #22: Inspecting and Replacing Motor Start Relay, takes the start winding out of the circuit after the run winding has engaged.

Note: When replacing motor, also replace the motor start relay to prevent premature failure of new motor.

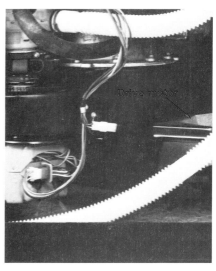

Drive motor

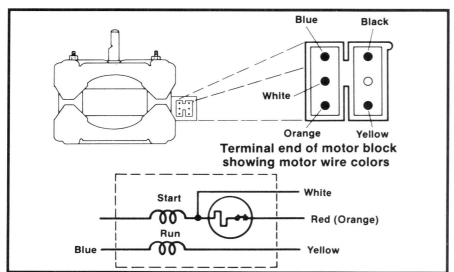

Terminal end of motor block showing motor wire colors

Drive motor terminal locations (colors designate wires between motor receptacle and motor windings, not harness windings.)

Step 1: Be sure all washer controls are turned **OFF**. Unplug the washer from the receptacle. Watch for sharp edges on access panels and parts.

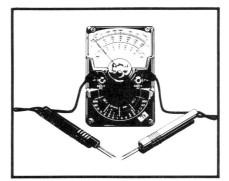

Step 2: This procedure requires the use of an ohmmeter. For instructions on how to use an ohmmeter, refer to Tools and Testing Equipment, page 101.

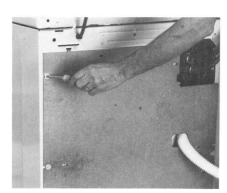

Step 3: Remove rear access panel and locate drive motor. If you are unfamiliar with removing the rear access panel, refer to Procedure #5: Removing Rear Access Panel.

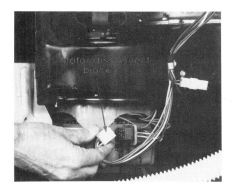

Step 4: Unplug plastic motor disconnect block.

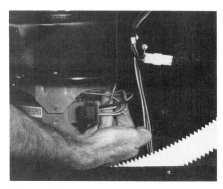

Step 5: Using drawings at beginning of this procedure, locate start and run windings. Find colored motor wires in same circuit.

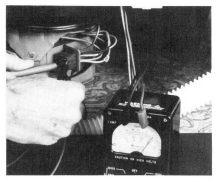

Step 6: Set ohmmeter at R x 1. Test start windings by touching one probe to black wire terminal and one to orange. Needle should sweep upscale, indicating continuity.

Step 7: Test run winding with ohmmeter by touching one probe to blue wire terminal and one to yellow. Needle should sweep upscale to 0, indicating continuity.

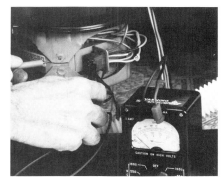

Step 8: Set ohmmeter for R x 100. Check for grounds by touching one probe to either black or orange terminal and one to motor case. Needle should remain downscale.

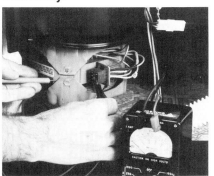

Step 9: Check for grounds by touching one probe to either blue or yellow terminal and one to motor case. Needle should remain downscale. If any ohmmeter tests fail, replace motor.

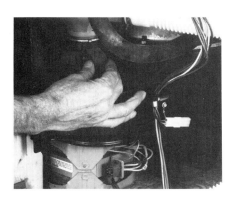

Step 10: Rotate flexible pump coupling in either direction to be sure motor is free to turn.

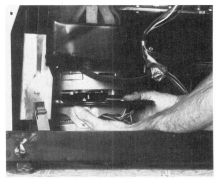

Step 11: To remove and reinstall motor, refer to either Procedure #27: Inspecting and Replacing Single Speed Clutch or Procedure #28: Inspecting and Replacing Two-Speed Clutch. Motor and clutch must be removed together, and clutch must be completely disassembled to replace motor.

Step 12: Reassemble washer and reconnect power supply.

31 Cosmetic repairs

Skill Level Rating:	Easy	Average	Difficult	Very Difficult

Your General Electric or Hotpoint washer can be kept attractive and new-looking by following maintenance instructions in your *Use and Care Book*. Applying a coat of appliance polish at least twice a year will also help protect your appliance against rust.

Through accidents or damage in moving, your appliance may need more extensive cosmetic repairs. Porcelain patch kits, spray paint and touch-up pencils can all be used. Be sure to carefully follow all directions that come with the product and use only in a well-ventilated area.

Note: Be sure to use the complete and correct model identification number when purchasing parts or paint.

CAUTION: Paint is flammable. Always paint in a well-ventilated area. Read all instructions on paint container carefully. Do not allow paint to contact plastic surfaces.

Matching touch-up paint is available for repairing scratches

31 continued

Step 1: For your personal safety, exercise caution when working with any electrical appliance. Spray paint in well-ventilated area.

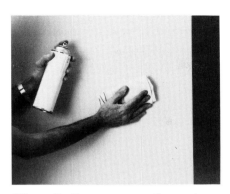

Step 2: To remove soil, wash with liquid household detergent, warm water and soft cloth. Remove all traces of wax and dirt and rinse with clear water before attempting to repair scratches.

Porcelain lid

Porcelain cover

Step 3: Your washer's cover and lid are made of porcelain. A porcelain patch kit can be purchased locally to repair scratches on cover or lid.

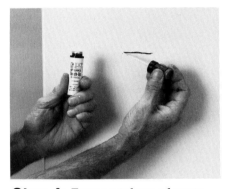

Step 4: Every surface of your washer except the cover and lid is painted. Small scratches can be repaired with touch-up pencil, which can be purchased from your authorized local appliance parts dealer. Or, spray small amount of spray paint into cap of can. Dip torn end of paper match into it and carefully fill in scratch.

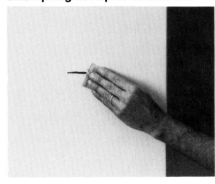

Step 5: Sand large scratches smooth with extra-fine sandpaper. Sand scratch until edge is "feathered" smoothly into exposed metal. Area to be painted must be clean, dry and free of grease or rust.

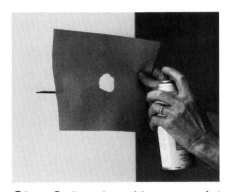

Step 6: Practice with spray paint before applying. Read and follow instructions on can. Spray area through irregular hole in piece of paper. Do not aim first spray at damaged area. Sweep across from masked area first. Use several coats to avoid running.

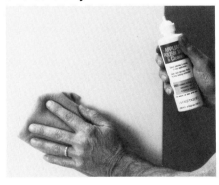

Step 7: Allow paint to dry thoroughly and wax with appliance polish, which can be purchased from your authorized local appliance parts dealer.

Technical assistance/Service record

This page is provided as a convenient reference for important washer repair information. There are spaces for you to record your washer model number, parts needed, repair notes (such as where wire leads reattach), and when repairs were made. There are also spaces for you to write down the phone numbers of your nearest GE and Hotpoint parts dealer and Factory Service Center.

Another important phone number for repair information belongs to The GE Answer Center® consumer information service. If you have difficulty in making any repair described in this book you can contact The GE Answer Center® consumer information service by calling 800-626-2000 toll free. The trained service professionals will try to talk you through the problem step. It helps to write down your model number, what you have done, and what is causing you difficulty before calling.

Model number:_____

Parts or components needed:

_____

_____

Repair notes:

_____

_____

Service record:

_____

_____

Water shut-off valve location:_____

Fuse or circuit breaker location:_____

Size fuse required:_____

Phone number of
General Electric and Hotpoint
parts dealer:_____

Phone number of
General Electric and Hotpoint
Factory Service Center:_____

Preventive maintenance

At the General Electric Company, we're committed to your satisfaction. The basic do's and don'ts included in this section are our way of helping you obtain the best results from your General Electric or Hotpoint washer. The few minutes you invest in caring for your appliance properly can save you a great deal of time and trouble.

This section outlines basic precautions and simple maintenance routines that will help prevent the small problems that can lead to big repair jobs. Take a little time to read this part of the manual and follow the advice given.

Improving the performance of your washer

- Do not overload your washer. Wash permanent press and synthetic fabrics in smaller loads to maximize cleaning and minimize wrinkling.
- Sort loads by fabric, weight, and color.
- Read garment labels for washing instructions.
- Be sure the temperature of your hot water is above 80°F, preferably around 105°F.
- Use the highest phosphorus content water conditioner available for maximum water softening (if necessary with your water supply) and washability.
- Apply detergent or a pre-wash product to stains 30 minutes before washing. Soak heavily soiled clothing in a solution of detergent and water before washing.
- Food or cooking oils on your synthetic garments may cause stains which are virtually invisible as you begin to wash your clothes. If these stains are not completely removed in the wash, the oily spots may pick up dirt from the wash water. Then, they will become very visible, and you may think they were caused by the wash cycle itself. Follow instructions in your *Use and Care Book* for prevention and removal of these unusual stains.
- Your washer's *Instruction Sheet* and *Use and Care Book* give you detailed instructions and explanations for a variety of washer performance problems. The *Use and Care Book* covers sorting, treating, soaking, loading, detergents, hard water, stains, different fabrics and loads and assorted special laundry problems. It is a valuable aid to obtaining maximum effectiveness from your General Electric or Hotpoint washer.

Washer interior maintenance

- The porcelain in the tub is basically self-cleaning. Leave the lid open after washing to allow moisture to evaporate. Do not use harsh or gritty cleansers.
- New washers have a normal "new" odor during the first few usages. Other "off" odors can be caused by accumulated lint or deposits around the agitator or on the wash tub. After any particularly dirty load, it may be necessary to immediately wipe out the tub.
- Remove lint and any foreign objects from the filter pan after each wash load.
- To remove limestone deposits from a clogged filter pan, follow the instructions in your *Use and Care Book*.
- Remove and lubricate the agitator every four to six months as recommended by your *Use and Care Book*. Accumulated lint and deposits around the agitator can cause "sour" odors. Agitator can be pulled straight off. Remove any accumulated lint. If slotted section at the top of the metal shaft appears dry, apply a light coat of petroleum jelly before replacing agitator. Make sure agitator "snaps" in place when replacing.

Washer exterior maintenance

- Never permit anyone to climb or stand on the washer; damage or injury could result.
- Wipe off any spilled laundry products as soon as possible using a damp cloth. Keep stain remover or pre-soak products away from your washer as these can damage outside surfaces.
- Do not use harsh or gritty cleaners. Clean control panel with a glass cleaner or a damp soft cloth.
- Keep sharp objects away from the surface of your washer.

General Maintenance Tips

- To store your washer, contact an authorized factory service technician to remove water from the drain pump and hoses to prevent freezing.
- For long vacations, be sure water supply is shut off at faucets and drain all water from the hoses if the temperature will be below freezing. Also, hydrogen gas can be produced and can build up in a water heater if you have not used hot water for a period of two weeks or more. HYDROGEN GAS CAN BE EXPLOSIVE UNDER THESE CIRCUMSTANCES. To prevent possible damage or injury, run hot water from the kitchen faucet for several minutes before using your washer. If the gas is present, you may hear a slight hissing or sputtering noise from the faucet. Do not smoke or allow any open flame near the faucet at this time.
- To move your washer, contact an authorized factory service technician to have washer crated to protect the suspension system and cabinet.

Tools and testing equipment

Tools

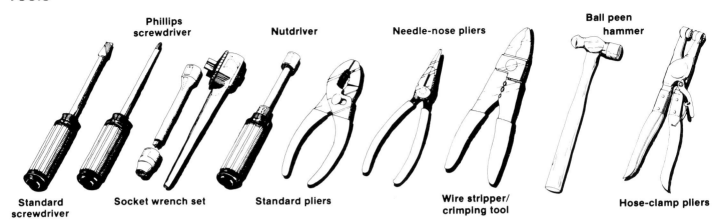

Phillips screwdriver

Nutdriver

Needle-nose pliers

Ball peen hammer

Standard screwdriver

Socket wrench set

Standard pliers

Wire stripper/ crimping tool

Hose-clamp pliers

Chances are you already have some of the above tools in your home. For safety and efficiency reasons it is important to use the proper tools when making washer repairs. The tool you will use the most is the screwdriver. Various sizes of standard and Phillips screwdrivers will be necessary to remove the many screws on your washer.

Some screws and nuts, especially those used on access panels, have hexagonal heads with no slots. To remove these, you will need either a nutdriver or socket wrench. The nutdriver is made like a screwdriver but has a small socket on one end. This socket fits over the hex head of the screw or nut. It's used just like a screwdriver.

The socket wrench usually has a handle with a ratchet that can be set to tighten or loosen a nut, an extension, and various sockets. Sockets usually come in a set containing several sizes, but the quarter-inch size is most commonly used on the washer.

To use a socket wrench, place the socket on the nut and turn the handle counter-clockwise to loosen it. If it makes a clicking sound and does not turn, flip the ratchet lever to the opposite direction and loosen the nut.

If you have difficulty finding hose-clamp pliers, try an auto-motive part house. Hose-clamp pliers are rigid like standard pliers but have notched jaws to help clamps firmly.

Testing equipment

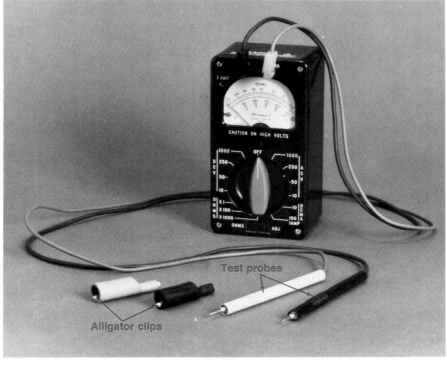

Test probes

Alligator clips

Ohmmeter

An ohmmeter is required to analyze the electrical workings of the electrical components of your washer. The ohmmeter is a simple device that measures the amount of resistance in an electrical circuit. Ohmmeters are usually combined with a voltmeter into an instrument called a multimeter, multitester, or volt-ohmmeters (VOM). Volt-ohm-meters can measure the amount of both resistance and voltage in an electrical circuit. A simple, inexpensive ohmmeter will be sufficient for any washer repairs presented in this manual.

Most problems that occur in an electrical circuit are invisible. For example, it is difficult to see contacts that are not closing inside a switch, or to find a break in a motor winding. For the most part, you'll be using the ohmmeter only as a continuity tester to determine whether or not electrical current can pass through the circuit. By passing a small electrical current from a battery contained inside the ohmmeter through the circuit, you can tell if the circuit is complete.

To understand the basic flow of electricity, think of it in terms of a water pumping station. In order for water to flow through the pipes, it must have a complete "closed loop" from the pump, through the valves, then back to the pump again. If the line is broken or opened at any point, water would eventually cease to flow.

The flow of electricity through your washer is similar to the pumping of water, except electrons rather than water are flowing through the circuitry. The pump is the washer plug-in receptacle that provides the force to circulate current through the washer circuits. The electrical circuit uses wires rather than pipes as the conductors of electricity and switches rather than valves to control the flow. Voltage is comparable to the pressure that exists in a water circuit, while electrical current could be compared to the flow rate of water that flows through the pipe.

meter gives you a choice of functions, select the range first, then "zero" the meter by touching the two test probes together. With the probes tightly in contact with each other, the needle of the meter should sweep towards "0" (zero) resistance. Now, while holding the probes together, adjust the knob marked "zero adjust" or "ohms adjust" until the needle rests directly over "0".

At this point, you can see exactly how the meter works. If instead of touching the probes together you touch them to each end of a wire, or to a fuse, the needle should sweep toward "0". This indicates that the

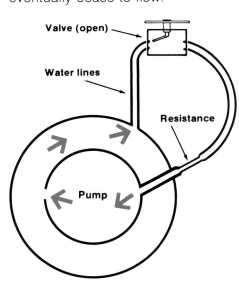

Valve (open)

Water lines

Resistance

Pump

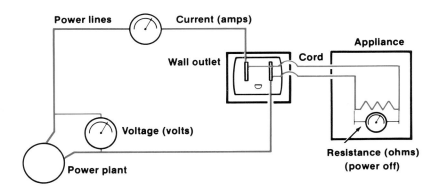

Power lines   Current (amps)

Wall outlet   Cord   Appliance

Voltage (volts)

Power plant

Resistance (ohms)
(power off)

Some tests with an ohmmeter will be needed for repair procedures presented in this manual. An ohmmeter will have either a switch or pair of jacks (plugs) that allow you to select the function of the meter. Resistance is measured in units called ohms and will be designated by the symbol Ω or the letter R. Your meter may have more than one range scale. When set at R x 1, the reading should be taken directly from the meter. When set at a higher scale, such as R x 100, the reading on the scale should be multiplied by 100 to obtain the correct resistance. Most measurements for testing components or circuits are made on the lowest scale, usually R x 1.

Plug the test leads in the jacks marked "ohms". The red lead goes in the positive (−) jack and the black on to negative (-). If your

wire or fuse will conduct electricity. But if the wire or fuse is broken inside, the needle would not move. When this condition exists in a component or circuit, it is said to be "open", and it cannot conduct electricity. But if the needle moves to indicate that it does conduct electricity, then the component or circuit is said to have "continuity".

All wires in the electrical circuit should indicate "0" resistance when tested in this manner. Switches should indicate "0" resistance when they're turned on, and should indicate maximum resistance when turned off. Components that do work will offer some electrical resistance, but will not be open. The meter reading for these instances should be somewhere between full scale and no reading.

Tools and testing equipment (cont.)

Many repair procedures in this manual advise you to test for grounds when checking a component. When doing this, you should select the highest resistance scale on the ohmmeter. You will be directed to place one test probe on a terminal of the component and the other test probe on a metallic portion of the component housing. No current should flow through those paths; if the meter indicates that continuity exists under those conditions, the component is grounded and should be replaced.

The repair procedures in this manual will show you the test points (where to place the test probes) for various tests. You'll find an ohmmeter to be a valuable addition to your home tool collection. For further information on the function and operation of the ohmmeter, see pages 99 and 100.

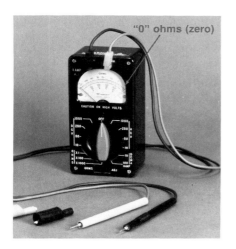

"0" ohms (zero)

Full-featured ohmmeters have numerous switch-selected ranges. Note that ohms scale at top is reversed – zero resistance is at full sweep of scale.

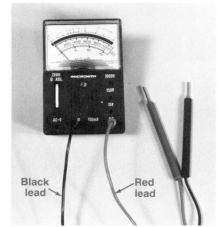

Black lead — Red lead

Inexpensive ohmmeters use jacks rather than switches to select function, but still provide zero ohms adjustment. Note that red lead plugs into positive (–) jack, black into negative (-) or common.

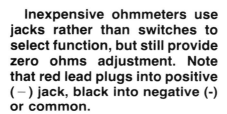

To zero ohmmeter, touch probes tightly together, turn zero adjustment knob until needle is centered over "0" (ZERO) at full sweep of scale. This adjusts readout to the battery condition and to the resistance selected.

Zero adjusting knob

Sometimes you can't identify a blown fuse, even when it has a glass shell. Saving a single service call for a simple problem like this can pay for the price of a meter.

Note: Digital ohmmeters do not use a multiplier. Select high, medium, or low range.

CAUTION: Do not attempt to test resistance of any circuit with the power turned on. Checking a live voltage circuit will result in damage to your testing meter.

Interpreting circuit diagrams and cam charts

Interpreting your washer's circuit diagram is not difficult once you know certain basic facts, symbols, and abbreviations. (Relevant symbols and abbreations are listed at the end of this section.) Wires are designated by colors to identify common circuits. All selector switch terminals (those you manually operate) are numbered. Your circuit diagram illustrates the path electricity follows as it enters your washer and flows through the timer behind your operating panel. The timer has a small motor and a cam which, according to its setting, activates the desired cycle. When a switch, or contact, is closed, electricity can flow uninterrupted. When a switch is open, the power may find another clear path. The cycles, times, and water levels you select tell the timer which "gate-ways" to open and which to close.

There are two types of timers used in General Electric and Hotpoint washers. Some have a plastic housing and some have a metal housing. Let's look closely at your circuit diagram. A cam chart accompanies it and will make its interpretation much simpler. There are some differences between the diagrams and charts for the two types of timers. Cam charts also differ from one washer model to another. We'll begin by looking at the plastic housing version.

Locate the switches at the left of the cam chart on your diagram. Number 1 is the motor switch, 3A is the main circuit switch, and 3B is used during the spin cycle, and when the water level switch is open and must be bypassed. Switches 4A and B control agitation, motor reversal, and spin. The middle section of your diagram illustrates these functions.

On the illustrated diagram, the switches are shown as they

Plastic housing timer circuit diagram

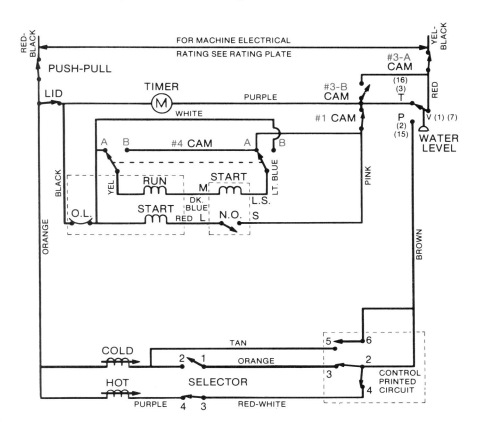

Plastic housing timer cam chart

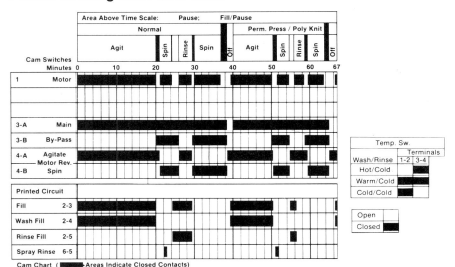

appear 10 minutes into the cycle. Using your cam chart, cover all areas of the cycle to the right of the 10 minute mark, and you will see the correspondence between the closed contacts on the chart and those on the diagram. If you suspect an electrical problem, using the cam chart in this way will show you instantly which switches should be closed (and conducting electricity at each point in the cycle) and which should be open.

102

Tools and testing equipment (cont.)

The circuitry and general location of switches on the metal housing timer circuit diagram are basically the same as with the plastic housing timer. However, the contacts are numbered and lettered differently, and certain symbols (identified beneath the diagram) differ. There is no main circuit switch on this timer. Those switches performing comparable functions, as explained for the plastic housing timer are noted on the illustration of the metal housing timer circuitry. Switches are pictured as they appear 12 minutes into the cycle. The cam chart is read in exactly the same way as the plastic housing timer chart.

Metal housing timer circuit diagram

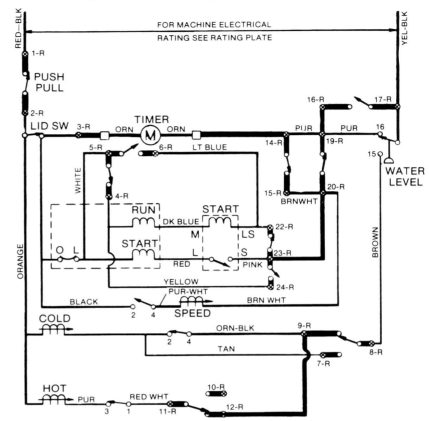

NOTE: CONTROL SWITCHES IN CIRCUIT DIAGRAM ARE SHOWN SET AT 12 MIN. TIME ON THE CAM CHART MANUAL SWITCHES ARE SHOWN SET FOR WARM WASH, COLD RINSE, AND NORMAL WASH, SPIN SPEED. NUMBERS AND LETTERS INDICATE CORRESPONDING COMPONENT TERMINAL DESIGNATIONS. HEAVY LINES INDICATE BUSSING INSIDE TIMER.

Temp. Sw.		
Wash	Terminals	
Rinse	2-4	3-1
Hot Cold		■
Warm Cold	■	
Cold Cold	■	

Action Sw.	
Wash	Terms.
Spin	2-4
Normal Fast	
Gentle Slow	■

Open	
Closed)	■

Metal housing timer cam chart

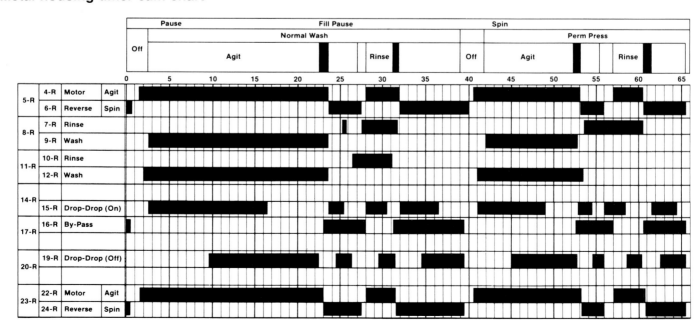

Symbols

The following Legend of Symbols and Abbreviations will assist you in
reading the circuit diagrams.

BUZZER		MOTOR WINDING	
FUSE		SWITCH OR CONTACT	
HEATING UNIT		WATER LEVEL SWITCH	
MOTOR		WATER SOLENOIDS	
OVERLOAD		WIRES CONNECTED	
RELAY		WIRES CROSSING	
RESISTOR			

Abbreviations

RLY - RELAY

SW - SWITCH

WDG - WINDING

WLS - WATER LEVEL SWITCH

Washer accessories

In addition to supplying quality original replacement parts for your washer, General Electric also provides a variety of useful home laundry accessories. Some accessories are replacement items that help keep your appliance looking and working like new, while others let you add new convenience features. The most popular and widely available washer accessories are featured below.

Appliance paint

High quality paints in spray cans and touch-up applicators are available in five colors to match General Electric and Hotpoint appliances. Camouflaging most nicks and scratches, appliance paint is an easy-to-use and long-lasting way to improve your washer's appearance.

Appliance wax and cleaner

Protective liquid wax contains silicone sealant to clean, polish and wax in one easy step. The 8-oz. squeeze bottle contains enough liquid wax for several applications to keep your washer finish in like-new condition.

WR97X216

Lint filter

Easy-to-clean filters remove lint from recirculating wash and rinse water to help keep clothes cleaner. Filters also distribute powdered bleach and detergents evenly through wash load.

WH1X2254 (9 ¼″ diameter)
WH1X2253 (11-½″ diameter)

Fabric softener dispenser

Automatically dispenses fabric softener rinse agent at the right time without guesswork when loaded at the beginning of wash. Helps reduce static electricity, minimize wrinkles, and make clothes softer.

WH47X39

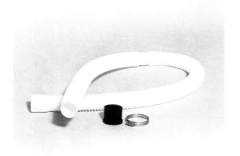

Drain hose extension

Allows convenient washer placement. Easy to attach to existing drain, flexible styrene drain hose is 44″ long and comes complete with coupling and clamp.

Fill hose

Replacement hoses feature built-in coupling and leak-resistant gasket for easy attachment to water lines. Hoses can be used for either hot or cold water supply.

Glossary of terms

Agitator coupling
An aluminum/rubber insert pressed into the inside of the agitator.

Backsplash
Control housing on top of washer.

Basket
Container inside washer where clothes are loaded and washed.

Bearing
Device that supports, guides, and reduces friction between fixed and moving parts.

Bell connector
Solderless connector for splicing wiring. Insulating cover crimps onto ends of wires to assure solid connection.

Belt
Continuous band of flexible material that transfers motion or power from one pulley, or shaft, to another.

Boss
Raised knob or bump that acts as guide or stop.

Cam chart
Chart showing which switches are opened and closed in timer at various points in washing cycle.

Cam (molded face)
Rotating surface with rises and falls that opens and closes switches in timer.

Cam (printed circuit)
Flat rotating surface with metallic foil that opens and closes switches in timer.

Circuit
Path of electrical current from power supply through wiring to point of use and back to source.

Circuit breaker
Device to protect circuit from current overload. "Tripped" circuit breaker interrupts circuit when current exceeds specified amount. See also FUSE.

Circuit diagram
Drawing using standard symbols to represent path of current from power supply through switches and components and back to source. Shows how wiring is connected between components and how internal wiring of components is arranged.

Closed (circuit)
Complete circuit which can conduct electricity.

Component
An individual electrical or mechanical part of a washer system.

Connector
Any device on the end of a wire to facilitate either connection or disconnection.

Contact
Switch component which opens and closes to complete or break an electrical circuit.

Continuity
Ability of circuit to conduct electricity.

Defective
In this manual, used to mean a component which does not function properly and which must be replaced.

Detent pin
U-shaped plastic or metal piece which holds control knob to timer shaft.

Distribution panel
Fuse or circuit breaker box that distributes incoming power from outside line into a number of household circuits.

Energize
To supply electrical current for operation of electrical component.

Flange
Piece of protruding metal, plastic, etc. used for mounting purposes or support.

Fuse
Device to protect circuit from current overload. "Blown" fuse automatically interrupts circuit when current exceeds specified amount. See also CIRCUIT BREAKER.

Gasket
Flexible material designed to provide water-tight seal between components or parts of washer body.

Ground
Connection to earth or to another conducting body which transmits current to earth. Metal components in a circuit must be grounded to prevent their accidentally becoming electrically charged, causing injury.

Housing
Plastic or metal casing that covers a component.

Impeller
Rotating blade inside pump chamber which moves water.

Inoperative
In this manual, used to mean a component which does not function, but which can be checked and possibly repaired.

Insulation
Material which does not conduct electricity. Used to separate current-carrying wires or components from other metal parts of the washer.

Lead (wire)
Portion of electrical wiring attached to component.

Leaf (switch)
Flexible metal portion of switch containing contacts.

Motor protector
Thermal protector inside drive motor which shuts motor down if motor gets too hot.

Nutdriver
Tool used to remove and reinstall hexagonal-head screws or nuts. Resembles a screwdriver with a small socket at the end instead of a blade.

Ohm
Measurement unit for electrical resistance.

Ohmmeter
Battery-operated test instrument for determining the continuity of a circuit and measuring its resistance.

Open (circuit)
Incomplete circuit which cannot conduct electricity.

Pulley
A wheel turned by or driving a belt.

Resistance
Restriction of current in an electrical circuit.

Short (circuit)
Accidentally created circuit between hot wire and any ground, allowing excessive current flow with little or no resistance.

Solenoid
Cylindrical coil of insulated wire that establishes a magnetic field in presence of current.

Speed nut
Sheet metal clip with embossed area to receive screw thread.

Switch
Device to turn current on and off in an electrical circuit.

Switch bank
Two or more switch leaves mounted in nonconductive block.

Terminal
Connection point between wiring and electrical components. Commonly used terminals in washers are push-on terminals, which are held in place by their snug fit.

Test probes
Metal components of ohmmeter which are attached to either end of a circuit during testing for continuity or resistance. See also OHMMETER.

Tub
Outer receptacle where the water is contained in washer.

Upscale
Reading from ohmmeter that indicates continuity in a circuit

Volt
Measurement unit for electrical pressure.

Watt
Measurement unit for electrical power.

Winding
One or more turns of wire forming a continuous coil for a relay or other rotating machine. A conductive path is formed by the wire.

Index

Index (cont.)